Every Duffer's Guide to Good Golf

BRIAN SWARBRICK

Comic illustrations by

BOB BUGG

Instructional illustrations by

VIRGINIA DEWART

Pelham Books

First published in Great Britain by
Pelham Books Ltd
52 Bedford Square
London WC1B 3EF
1973

ISBN 0 7207 0686 6

Printed in Great Britain by Compton Printing Ltd, Aylesbury, on paper supplied by P. F. Bingham Ltd and bound by Dorstel Press, Harlow

CONTENTS

Introduction

Quick, how many people do you know who play polo?

Well, that's how many people I remember as being golfers when I was a teen-ager, let's say 25 or 30 years ago. Golf then was still thought of as a rich man's game, almost a snob sport (right up there with tuna fishing and falconry), and definitely not the sort of thing to attract the average guy.

Today, all that has changed.

Millions of people play golf: short guys, tall guys, fat guys, rich guys, bookies and bankers, kids of 10 and patriarchs of 80, men and women—even people with considerable physical handicaps, like amputees and the blind. We still shy away from laying out the hundreds or even thousands of dollars to buy membership in a private club—but there is probably not a community in all of this vast continent so remote that it isn't within a 5-iron shot of at least one public course. And we don't even have to buy our own clubs, because the pro shops are happy to rent a set for a couple of dollars.

Yet, with everything made so easy for millions of us to take up the sport, only a small fraction of golf's multitudes have taken the time and trouble to learn to play the game. And that is a shame. Golf is a tremendous amount of fun when you know how to play it, and it can be bitterly frustrating when you don't.

What is golf all about?

Ken Harrelson summed it up pretty neatly in 1971 when he announced that he was going to quit baseball, and a salary of $70,000 a year, to take up tournament golf. People said he was a basket case to give up that kind of bread, but Harrelson responded thus: Baseball required five talents of him—to be able to run, catch, throw, hit, and think. Since all he could do was hit and think, he was turning in his bat for a No. 1 wood.

Hit and think.

That's what golf is all about, and that's what this book is all about: how to hit the ball and how to think your way around a golf course—and how to put those two elements together so that you come back to the clubhouse with a score no worse than bogey.

In the following chapters we'll be discussing the art and science of golf. And we'll be doing it step by step, a little at a time, so that you can get the hang of one lesson before starting out on the next.

From time to time you'll begin to suspect you're being spoon-fed. But there's a good reason for it. Golf, as you'll read more than once in these pages, is not a particularly natural game. Like sword-swallowing, it has to be learned.

And on your way to learning it, you are going to encounter what may seem to be strange contradictions, especially contradictions of some of the pointers you have been given already by well-meaning friends.

It's not so much that their advice is faulty, but rather that it's all too often incomplete. If there are, let's say, seven components in a good grip, and a well-meaning friend gives you a tip on one without reference to the other six, the advice isn't worth a pinch. To play good golf—and believe me, bogey is good golf—you must know how to do *everything* right. It's the little mental-physical lapse—knowing it but not always doing it quite right—which separates the bogey golfer from the scratch golfer. All of us have these lapses. If we didn't we'd all be out on the tournament trail with Jack and Lee and Arnie.

What I'm getting at is this: a thorough knowledge of all the parts is what makes the whole. And even when your mind knows it, you need actual practice to get the message to your body. Nobody I have ever met has been able to put it all together at once. You can be the greatest natural physical talent in the world, able on occasion to hit the little demon 300 yards or more—but if you don't know how you did it, if you can't step up and do it next time, and the time after that and the time after that, you'd be destroyed in a game against a solid bogey shooter who may never hit the ball more than 175 yards.

Doing it right, and knowing how you did it, and being able to do it shot after shot—that's golf.

With this in mind, each chapter in this book takes apart one of the mysteries of golf and discusses it in detail. Then, at the end of the chapter, there's a summary of all the main points of the instruction. This is intended to get you in the habit of focusing your mind on a single golfing problem and the various components that go into solving that problem.

Think of each chapter as a lesson, a lesson guaranteed to save you at least one stroke in every round. Be content to learn that lesson thoroughly, and try to avoid what I think is a natural impulse—to try to gobble up the whole book at once and then go out and challenge your club champion.

Above all, don't become despondent if there is no immediate improvement in your game. The mind is sometimes reluctant to send the message down to the body. You have to practice each instruction until your body starts telling you that it feels right. Because it will, you know. Ask any good golfer. He *knows* when he's swung right; his whole body says so.

Don't give up early, either, if an instruction in this book doesn't feel right the first dozen or so times you try it. As

I've said, hitting a golf ball is not a particularly natural exercise, and it calls for all kinds of little physical departures from say, the movements of swinging an ax or hitting a baseball. Take my word for it: if you've learned the instruction properly, the feeling of awkwardness goes away quickly... like, the instant you smash the ball out of sight.

If some instruction seems to be particularly slow in producing results, go back to the chapter and read it over carefully. In all of us there's the temptation to brush aside some odd little point which we don't completely understand, on the assumption that it probably isn't all that important.

Maybe it isn't—but a man who shoots 120 may not be the best judge of what's important, either. And remember, when one of those $100,000 a year tournament pros sends a bad shot into the woods and blows first-place money, it's because he forgot some "odd little point."

Finally, any book of general instruction has a problem in trying to define its "average reader." I have not been able to do so, beyond the arbitrary assumption that you have played the game at least a few times and that your score is nothing to write home about. Thus, you'll find odd bits of information for fat golfers or extraordinarily tall golfers, or odd sidelights about rules and etiquette, or tips on exercises, none of which may apply directly to you. Bear with me through these sections, please.

Better yet, tell your fat friends to buy the book.

What Price Jack Nicklaus?

Let's approach this thing with all the ugly facts in plain view.

Your game stinks, right?

If you play an easy course which you know pretty well, you can stagger around in 105 to 125 blows, and once or twice a year you break The Magic Hundred by a stroke or so. But if you play a fairly tough course, or even one that you're simply not familiar with, your score soars higher than your I.Q.

And yet, when you go out to a driving range, you're not that bad. In fact, in your own modest assessment, some of those shots you left on the driving range would turn you in with a very creditable 85 or so, if only you could execute them on an actual course. Perhaps not the first ten or eleven balls you hit, but the stuff you occasionally tag once you get the groove of your swing.

Yup. You're right. Your game stinks.

Well, I hate to have to put it so bluntly, but if you think you're going to play like Jack Nicklaus when you've digested *The Duffer's Guide,* forget it. I will hazard an early guess, without knowing anything more about you than that you're a duffer—and on the assumption that you are older than 25—that you will never hit the ball 300 yards, and you will never break 70.

Sure, your game stinks—but then, Jack Nicklaus used to shoot in the 100s, too. He was about six at the time.

Neither will I. Neither will all but the tiniest fraction of the more than ten million people, both male and female, who now play golf in North America.

Before that bleak prospect gives you a trauma, consider Ted Williams and his awesome talents with a baseball bat. When he was averaging .400, he was the greatest hitter in the game. Yet that fantastic .400 meant that even the mighty Williams, with all his superlative skill, could do it right only four out of ten times.

Think of golf in the same light. To hit a ball 300 yards is an almost incredible feat. So is breaking 70. If these are your goals, I suggest you marry a rich widow, take up residence on a golf course, and start buying lessons from the pro at the rate of about seven hours a day, seven days a week. If you're under 25, with that rare combination of the right physical and mental endowments, you just might make it. Four or five years from now.

Oh, sure, there are the occasional exceptions. I know a Toronto lawyer who never hefted a club until he was 50, yet today, approaching 60, he has a handicap in the single numbers and he can still poke a ball out of sight. How does he do it? I don't think even his teaching pro could give you a precise explanation. But my own appraisal is that this gaffer combines three special ingredients: he has the coordination and muscularity of a much younger man, he has a fierce determination to excel at everything he tries—and he has the time and bank balance to afford all those lessons.

Now, how about you? You are the only one who really knows: How fierce is your determination? Is it desperately important to you to hit 300 yards and make a shambles of par?

I doubt it. Far more likely, what you really want to do is play 18 holes and not feel like an idiot when you come off the course.

Naturally, as you begin to feel your game improving, the targets you set for yourself get progressively tougher. But right now what you'd really like—and more important, what you are willing and able to work toward—is to get your card down to a fairly consistent 88 or 90 strokes per round. In other words, bogey golf.

If I have described you accurately—if, all fantasy aside, this is your immediate goal—then *The Duffer's Guide* can help you.

But there is one constant truism you *must* keep in mind. Golf, to be perfectly frank about it, is not an easy game to learn. It's tough, it's frustrating, and there just aren't any shortcuts. The advice in this *Guide* will help you only if you take the trouble to make sure you really understand it. If you're anything like me, there are times when you're reading with only half your mind. If you find yourself in that mood, put the *Guide* down until another time. There is no profit in giving perfunctory attention to a lesson; it must be fully absorbed by the mind before it can be executed by the body.

Let me restate this important point another way. Understanding what it is that you are doing wrong is difficult, far more difficult than the physical task of correcting the mistake. You don't have to be a contortionist to execute a good golf swing, but you have to get it right in your head first before it becomes second nature to your body.

Don't go leaping ahead to the middle chapters to find out how to blast a ball into next week. You may never be able to boom it out of the cannon—and trying to do so is probably one of the key reasons why so many people never get their score south of 100.

Take it easy and go page by page, building up a little library in your head of the philosophy of the game and the physics involved in a golf shot. Don't just *read* the playing hints you find here; think them through, work at the exercises outlined in later chapters, commit them to memory, and resolve to put them to work the next time you're out on an actual course.

Most Duffers Remain So Because They Have No Real Interest in Becoming Golfers

Nobody likes to admit to that shortcoming, but it's an affliction which hits even the keenest, most fanatical golfers. They love to play, but somehow they get short-circuited when it comes to learning how to play well.

I was once the same way. For a period of ten years my scorecards usually ranged between 110 and 120. So did those of my playing partner. Then, at the end of that tenth season a light went on in my head. All of the mistakes I had been making for years came into sharp focus. Precisely how it happened (and how it can happen for you) is described in Chapter Two, but for the moment let's look at my breakthrough from the other side—the fact that it didn't happen to my partner.

We had played through the tenth season as duffers. By the end of the first month of the eleventh season I had shed between 20 and 30 strokes from my average score, and he was still shooting 110-120. I told him how much my game had improved, and naturally he didn't believe me. He wanted proof. So out we went for our first game of the season together.

The first thing I noticed, which had never occurred to me before, was that he stood so far back at address that he had to lean over in the most precarious stance just to get the toe of his club lined up behind the ball.

"Stand closer," I said. "Don't strain yourself."

"Shut up," he said. "You play your game, I'll play mine."

Whack! He hit the ball halfway to Yugoslavia.

Everybody knows what kind of look he gave me then, right? Triumph!

And it didn't diminish any when my own drive went out only 205 yards or so, almost 40 yards short of his. Nor was he particularly perturbed when I holed out in bogey 5, and he took a double bogey 6. After all, he had creamed me off the tee.

The second hole was a short par 4, only 320 yards. Its

Ah, pity the poor duffer here, folks. Somehow he has picked up the notion that the farther you can get from the ball at address, the mightier the stroke you can give it. But consider this: If you have to lean over, off-balance, just to address the ball, you may not even hit it at all on the actual swing. Without crowding yourself, aim for the most compact stroke your physical potential allows.

only difficulty was a river on the right and a little wooded mound on the left which pinched the fairway into a narrow slot about 200 yards out. I used a 3 iron and landed close to the slot, with an easy shot to the open green.

"A little chicken today, are we?" he said, lining up to his ball with the big stick in hand.

"You're still standing too far back," I said. "And the shot's too dangerous for a driver."

"Are you going to keep up the helpful hints all the way around?"

"You wanted to know how I got my score down," I said. "One way was to learn not to take chances."

Silence. He stays with his driver. He doesn't move closer to the ball. He swings.

Whiff.

He misses completely.

More silence. I am not about to get my head ripped off by uttering *anything* at this point. In fact, I don't even look in his direction until I hear his clubface hit the ball. Then we both watch the ball. We watch it on the fly, we watch it on the first bounce, we watch it on the second bounce, and then we're unable to watch it any more because it goes straight into the woods. And after five minutes of searching that's where we find it. Nestled against the root of a tree. Unplayable.

My friend took a 6 on that hole, which was pretty nifty, considering he had two penalty strokes, I took a very unspectacular 4.

Now, this guy was no dummy. As the game progressed and I pulled steadily away from him, he knew I had something going for me, something which continued to elude him, and we started to talk about it. At least we started to talk about my game, because he refused to even consider any change in his own.

"Look," he said, "some guys like putting, some guys like chipping, some guys like fairway woods. I like driving. I like to crack the big one out there. And as long as I can outdrive you—"

"When you don't miss it completely."

"Okay, but when I *do* get hold of it—"

"—it's because you have good coordination and balance and you can frequently overcome the handicap which that stance is giving you. All you're really doing," I said, "is achieving a desirable factor, a good extension in your swing, by an undesirable, artificial means."

He was unconvinced, but he said he was willing to try "crowding the ball" (which, of course, was not what I had suggested) if it would make me happy.

"Uh-uh," I said, knowing even in those days that a golf course is where you go to play golf; the practice range is where you go to experiment.

Instead, I suggested that this outing concern itself with what I call Realistic Assessment, a rather classy term for simply using your head. My friend seemed to be in utter agreement with me as to the part it played in improving one's score. To hear him tell it, if there was anybody who knew how to play canny, heads-up golf, he was that fella. (Which meant, of course, that he had neatly managed to forget about that second hole.)

There was no opportunity to put him to the test again until we reached the twelfth hole. It was barely a par 4, measuring only 280 yards. Moreover, it had a little dogleg to the right, which was slight enough that you could still see the green from the tee, but which reduced the practical yardage involved to only about 260.

A slight problem, however: about 160 yards out, just where the dogleg began, a stream meandered across the fairway from right to left, presenting a 20-yard water hazard from the 160-yard point on the right, angling off to the 200-yard mark on the left of the fairway. Bunkering around the green was arranged in such a way that anybody who felt like going for it in one had to be absolutely sure that he could fly the ball at least 200 yards just to miss the water, and still be on line to the green. In short, if you couldn't be sure of hitting it very long and very straight, there was no percentage in using a distance club. For a percentage shooter the hole definitely called for a lofted club to lay a shot short of the river and the same club to put the ball on the green. That's the way I played it, and I got a routine par 4.

My partner automatically hauled out the heavy artillery.

Realistic assessment had just gone out the window. He knew perfectly well that he couldn't drive the ball 260 yards, he knew perfectly well that he couldn't count on its going straight, and he had had plenty of evidence that something would likely go wrong and he would end up right in the drink. On top of that, he was then down about a dozen strokes and in no position to try something nutty.

"Yeah, yeah, I know. I just want to see, though. I got a feeling."

Well, just to keep you off the edge of your chair, naturally it went right into the river. And what did he say to that? Did he admit he'd been unrealistic?

"Wow, two yards, that's all it needed, just another two lousy yards!"

Oh, yes, I know all too well how powerful that go-for-broke urge can be, and I am sympathetic. But at the same time, this is a book about how to play better golf, and realistic assessment of each golfing situation plays a big part in the instruction. If you are tempted to try something which you know perfectly well is 99.9 percent doomed to failure, you must exercise iron discipline to resist that temptation.

My friend couldn't resist temptation because he didn't really want to become a good golfer. He wanted to be a long hitter. And he's still a pigeon for anyone who can break 100.

Agreed, at some time during every big tournament we read about one of the superstars "going for broke"—but when they use that expression, they don't mean it the way you and I do. They mean that their situation has become critical and it demands attempting a very risky shot—but one which they damn well know is within their capability.

In short, pros take occasional chances, duffers take foolish chances.

This business of realistic assessment is a broad concept, and I'll admit, somewhat abstract, but if you can get the basic philosophy going for you, you're well on your way to saving strokes.

In one respect, I suppose it can be said that you have already put the concept to work. You have picked up this book, which promises only to guide you to bogey golf; this shows that you are realistic enough to realize (assess) that you are not yet in the bogey class, and that shooting one-over-par on every hole is a reasonable primary target for your present abilities.

Here is an example of failure to make realistic assessments.

A few years ago I showed up at the first tee of a little nine-hole public course. It was early morning, and I'd hoped to play the round by myself, to sort out a few things that needed work. However, there was another lone golfer on the tee; he suggested I join him, and off we went.

Now, get the picture. This man and I had never seen each other before, we were not likely to see each other again, and we were not playing for money.

Between us, nothing whatever was at stake.

Okay, off we go.

I took a 6 on the first hole, a par 4 dogleg to the right from a tremendously elevated tee. It was about 180 yards to the turn, and I wanted to find out if I could make it with my 3 iron. I could not. I was just short, but it still took a stroke to get around the corner, a third to get alongside the green, a fourth to chip on, and with two putts, there was my 6.

As I jotted it down, I asked my stranger-partner how many strokes he had taken. While I had not been paying strict attention, I had a hazy awareness that he had needed eight bashes to get within two feet of the hole and had then picked up, apparently under the impression that a gent like myself would automatically award a gimmee on two-footers. I do not, but what the hell?

"Oh," he said, "about the same as you. A 6, I think." *About* the same? What kind of mathematics is that?

However, he looked me squarely and innocently in the eye as he said this, and since it mattered nothing to me, I marked us each with a 6. From then on, though, I kept a close mental record of the strokes he took. On the first four holes, by his reckoning the man had scored a 6, 7, 7, 8; by actual count he was 9, 9, 9, 8.

If we had been wagering, there might be some explanation, however scurrilous, for shaving seven strokes from his actual score. But I don't think this man was trying to fool me. He was trying to kid himself.

He simply refused to realistically assess his own lousy golf. He had somehow convinced himself that it was easier to tell a little white lie to the scorecard than it was to buckle down, cut out the nonsense, and learn how to play better.

And the sad thing was, with any amount of self-discipline, he had the makings of a not-bad golfer. Physically, there was no reason why he couldn't get down to quite respectable high 80s golf, but he will probably never get there. For all I know, he may never have finished that round. When I left him at the fifth hole, he had suspended his interest in golf in favor of hunting along a river bank for lost balls.

I learned two things from this incident, in terms of realistic assessment.

The first was a reminder never to kid myself into overlooking shots when marking my score, no matter how much I might argue that "that-one-really-shouldn't-count." Come on, guys, they *all* count! It is only by facing up to duffed shots that we resolve to conquer them next time. If we don't count them, they get pleasantly hazy in the memory, and we never learn.

This also applies, of course, to the gent who gets into the double numbers somewhere in the first few holes and refuses after that even to keep score. (Please keep in mind that whenever I criticize some hypothetical golfer, I am really talking about little old me; all of these bad habits once were mine.) Sure, it knocks the stuffing out of your image of yourself as another Arnold Palmer to have to pencil in a 10 or 11 or 12, but only by marking it in and resolving to bear down for the rest of the round will you ever learn that disaster can be overcome.

Imagine yourself on a par-70 course in which the first hole is a par 3, 160 yards, with a huge pond running almost from tee to green. Let's say you are stricken with calamitous misadventure and you fire your first two or three into the pond. By the time you finally hole out, you are counting 12. Ghastly! But somehow you press on, putting disaster behind you, and complete the round by shooting no worse than bogey on each of the remaining 17 holes.

What would your score be? 105? 110? Uh-uh. Nowhere near it. By bearing down and forgetting the first hole, you would have managed a very creditable final score of 96.

My second discovery from the outing with the mathematician was that it took me more than a 3 iron to reach a dogleg 180 yards out. It matters nothing that the super-athletes of TV golf get that kind of distance out of their 6 iron; I need more club. And this is the basis of a very important lesson: If ten players in a row precede you to the tee, and they all use a 5 iron, and they all make a perfect shot—and you know in your heart of hearts that you can't possibly match their shot with anything less than a 3 wood, then for goodness' sake, leave the iron in the bag and go with the wood. Never let anyone else's ability influence your own realistic assessment of your own game. This is a game of golf, not a long-hitting competition. The man who can place his ball in the right spot to make the next shot is the man who's going to win—even if he has to use a howitzer to do it while all about him are using Ping-Pong paddles.

And this is the straight goods: lots of men who can hit the ball a mile still can't break 100.

The duffer finds this very difficult to believe. He is sure that all will be well with his game if only he can learn how to get that ball 250 yards straight down the middle. This isn't so, and I'll prove it to you later, but in this first chapter let's confine ourselves to a little mental warm-up on the general philosophy of the game.

See if this situation fits you:

A few years back I was playing a public course with a young Scotsman, a hotel chef whose work left him with free afternoons which, he told me, he was determined to spend getting his game into shape. I had started out playing immediately behind him, by myself again, and it was obvious by the fourth hole that his determination was not going to be enough. He was a real hacker. His shots would skitter about 60 yards, and he would slouch after them in steadily deepening dejection.

My own presence behind him, which by this time must have seemed to him to be casting a long, accusing shadow, was making things no easier. When he reached the fourth green, having taken seven or eight strokes to get there, he looked back and waved me to play up. From about 150 yards out I had a little magic moment and laid a 5 iron dead to the stick. I putted out with him, and we decided to head onto the fifth as a twosome.

"I'm sorry I didn't wave you up earlier," he apologized. "I'm playing so badly today it's not fair to hold up anybody behind me."

I said something like, "Oh, forget it. I've got lots of time," and didn't think anything more about it until later, when I was going over my notes for *The Duffer's Guide.* Then I realized I had missed the whole point.

Friend, it is not the players behind you who have lots of time, it is you. Time to get your nerves steadied after a bad shot. Time to get your breathing settled after lugging your clubs down the fairway. Time to spend a few seconds—not five minutes, but at least a few seconds—deliberating which club the next shot requires. And don't try to speed things up by trying to resolve your deliberations while you're still 20 yards from your ball. It takes an expert to do that—and experts don't do it. Wait till you're standing at the spot from which you'll shoot before trying to assess the distance to the green.

(I told you in the Introduction that you would come up against contradictions. Here's one of them. Although I make my final decision as to the proper club only when I am standing beside the ball, I have developed the habit, in approach-shot situations, of looking at the green as I walk toward it and thinking about a par 3 hole I know very well which requires, let's say, a 5 iron. When I get to that point on the fairway which has the exact feel of the known 5-iron situation, I say to myself, "Right, it would be a 5 from here." Then, as I get

Hey, hey, what's the rush? It's all that hurrying to try to get out of the way of following players that's making you duff those shots. Practice reasonable etiquette, but remember that you have as much right to concentrate on every stroke as the next guy—and you can't do that if you get to worrying about somebody behind you.

closer, "A 6 from here," and so on until I get to the ball. It's a judgment aid I've developed to minimize those moments when you stand at the ball and say, "Damn, I've got *no* idea what to use!")

Back to taking your time. The philosophy is this: By taking your time and giving yourself a chance to get a good shot away, you get out of the range of following players a damn

sight faster than if you allow yourself to become so preoccupied by *their* need to hurry (which, after all, is strictly their problem) that you address the ball unprepared and render one of the more ghastly strokes in your repertoire.

Oh, and doesn't that thought raise some ugly memories!

How often have I stood at the tee with another foursome right behind me—usually with at least one of them taking wind-whistling practice swings almost at my ear—and me so rattled with an impending sense of doom and a clear knowledge of my own inadequacy . . . that I missed the ball completely.

What's that you say? You're still doing that?

All right, here's the ideal place to apply golf philosophy. Obviously, the trick is to be able to concentrate so strongly on the business at hand that you're able to blank out the distractions around you. But let's suppose you didn't, and your miserable poop from the tee has placed you only 90 yards down the fairway. As you approach the ball, you know the following foursome is at the tee, silently but impatiently shrieking, "Get on with it, you palsied boob!" So you rush your second shot in your hurry to accommodate them, and it lurches no more than 60 or 70 yards further along.

Oh, the mortification! The embarrassment, the frustration, the welling agony of fury with your own ineptitude!

Now: Stop cold. Look back. See how far the following foursome hit *their* tee shots.

Ahhh, yes. There wasn't a reason in the world to hurry, was there? At least one of those guys—and maybe all four of them—sent the ball into the woods, kerplunk in a river, or off the tee in a puny dribble that didn't even reach your own opening blast.

What have you learned? Just this: Most players are as bad as you are.

The guy resplendent in the gold sweater, the chartreuse pants, the iguana skin golf bag, and the mink clubhead covers doesn't necessarily play any better than you. He's just richer than you are. You aren't going to hold him up by taking your time and thoroughly concentrating on getting a decent shot away.

A point to keep in mind is that if you're being crowded

from behind, it's a good bet that the chap doing the crowding is not a good golfer. In the first place, good golfers have a built-in antenna; they know which days and which hours a course is likely to be in heavy use, and they stay home. In the second place, if they do get caught in the crowd, they purposely lay back to open a space in front of them—because they know that if they start playing up somebody's back, their own game will suffer, too. And they have patient compassion for what you're going through. After all, they went through the same thing once.

A final note on realistic assessment. You'll find hundreds of stroke-saving applications of it once you start to think about it, but let these few examples alert your mind to the possibilities.

Picture two fairways running side by side with a dividing belt of trees between them. You are playing the fairway on the left, par 4, 400 yards. Your tee shot starts out with dignity, but it turns into a slice about 80 yards out and flies over the trees onto the adjacent fairway. Total distance forward, 130 yards.

You arrive at your ball and survey the situation. Ahead, on a straight line between you and the green, is the wall of trees. At about ten o'clock, however, the trees thin out and there is a nice 15-yard gap back to your own fairway. If you dump a little 7 iron in there, you'll have used up a shot, but you'll be back on your own fairway, with perhaps another 7 iron to the pin.

Now be honest (realistic) with yourself. Which shot would you *normally* attempt?

We all know that answer, don't we, duffers? Blast straight for the trees in the hope that they will magically open, like the Red Sea, and our ball will sail fairly to the green.

We also know that this never happens. We even know that if there were no trees, we still couldn't hit the ball far enough to reach a green 270 yards away, so even if we got through the

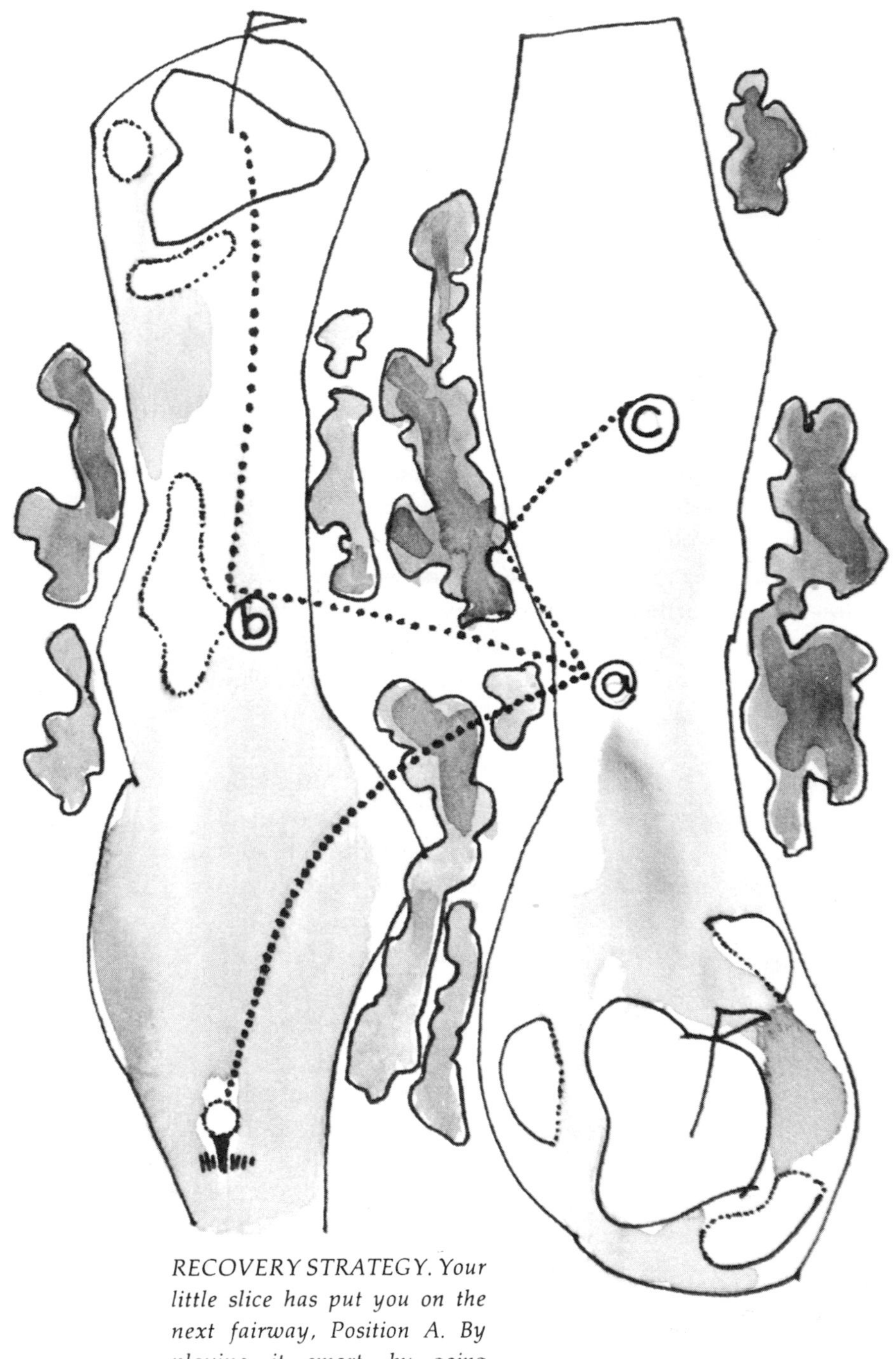

RECOVERY STRATEGY. Your little slice has put you on the next fairway, Position A. By playing it smart, by going through the opening and arriving at Position B, a bogey score is still possible. By playing it cute, odds are you'll hit the trees, land at Position C, and we may never see you again.

woods, there would still be a third shot to the green.

Ironically, we also know that if we were sitting around the clubhouse and somebody raised this subject for discussion, none of us would suggest the line drive into the trees. Someone might go for proceeding down the wrong fairway and then executing a recovery onto the green, but nobody would opt for the 100-to-1 miracle shot.

Yet as soon as we set foot on the course, logic deserts us. It isn't so much that we don't know what to do (as my speculation about the clubhouse discussion suggests), but that we refuse to do the obvious.

Yet look at how the obvious shot pays off:

First, to get back on your own fairway as soon as possible is clean golf. If you insist on playing dumb golf, you know it's dumb, and the chances are that just knowing you are attempting something silly will make you flub the shot and get into even worse trouble—like another slice, which may land you *two* fairways removed from where you want to go.

Second, a good recovery shot is precisely that, a good shot, and any time you execute a good shot it gives you a feeling of well-being and confidence which is a big plus factor in anybody's game.

Third, every time you realistically assess the situation and proceed to do The Right Thing, you are playing brainy, knowledgeable golf, and you know it. A few such assessments and you begin to feel that while you still may not be master of the game, you are no longer its befuddled slave.

Especially be realistic about unplayable lies. If your assessment tells you that the lie requires a miracle to recover from it, accept the penalty stroke and get your ball back on the fairway again. A good test of whether a lie is unplayable is to ask yourself whether you think your opponent could get the ball out of its difficulty. You may kid yourself that you can pull off a miracle, but you're probably more realistic about his ability—and if you know that he couldn't make the shot, accept that you can't make it either.

Sam Snead, by the way, is one of the golfing greats who is very reluctant to declare his ball unplayable. But before you side with Snead, let's examine not only his argument, but his armament.

Once, at Baltusrol, Snead found himself against a fence post, so tight that he couldn't play two-handed, and couldn't even play right-handed. So Snead took an 8 iron, reversed it, shot left-handed, and drove the ball 145 yards!

If you can do that, duffer, then by all means disregard my advice. But if you can't, get smart and accept the fact that it is better to lose one penalty stroke and get into the clear than to infuriate yourself by having to take two or three hacks at the pill before you're back on the fairway.

A bravery note: having taken the penalty, no further display of courage, fair play, and manliness is required. Make sure you drop that ball on the open stretch of fairway that your penalty paid for, and not on a spot that's almost as difficult as the one you were just in.

Well, here we are at the end of the first chapter, and I wonder how many of you are feeling that you have not learned one thing to improve your game. If so, good for you. It means your problems lie elsewhere than in the basic philosophy of the game, and we'll be getting to work on those problems shortly.

For the rest of you—the chaps who may now be sensing that they have been approaching the game all wrong—I calculate that this chapter should lop at least a half dozen strokes from your score. These are the "fatty tissue" strokes, the extra lard you should never have been handicapped with in the first place.

SUMMARY

1. Avoid that fatal fascination for the driver. There are 14 clubs in your bag, and it's just one of them. A preoccupation with trying to hit the ball out of sight almost always courts disaster.

2. Count every stroke, no matter how much it hurts. Just by knowing that everything counts, you "psych" yourself into playing the game seriously.
3. Use the club that gives you the best chance of getting the job done, no matter what you see others using, or no matter what the routine choice might indicate. Be realistic about your capabilities. There's no dishonor in needing more club than the other fellow. That old saying is really true: it's not how, it's how many.
4. Take your time with every stroke, and put the gallery out of your mind while you're making your shot. It is fantastically difficult to get a good shot away if your mind is on the people around you. And if you run up against a fellow who is doing something really distracting, just step away from your ball and look at him. That's usually enough to shut him up. But remember, once he's shut up, forget him completely.
5. Don't preselect your club. Wait till you are standing at the ball before hauling the weapon out of the bag.
6. Don't try to thread a recovery shot through an impenetrable forest. In this case, the shortest distance between two points is usually L-shaped.

Finally, commit the above to memory, and make it an automatic part of your game. Remember, to reach the top of a mountain, you have to start off by taking a step. In golf, using your head is Step One.

Whose Par Is Whose?

This is the chapter where I unveil the big secret: how to shave a couple of dozen strokes from your score simply by using your head.

But first, a few thoughts:

I think I read in the *Encyclopaedia Britannica* that "bogey" is a word coined from the surname of Colonel Bogey, who was reportedly able to tour a golf course in one stroke more per hole than par. You may be pleased and encouraged to know that in the opinion of *Britannica* the good colonel was a very fair hand with a stick.

I have also read in *Webster's Collegiate Dictionary* that "par" is "the number of strokes required for a hole or a round played perfectly . . . ."

Now isn't that an interesting word. *Perfectly*.

What does it mean, as far as golf is concerned? We all know that, reduced to its simplest terms, this is a game of distance and direction. Hit it straight enough, hit it far enough, and you achieve "par." But that still doesn't explain perfection. The direction part is easy: a straight line between tee and cup. But what about distance? Is there some magic distance which is perfection to achieve, all other distances being imperfect?

Not as far as I can find out.

Let us consider George Knudsen and Jack Nicklaus. Knudsen can belt them out as straight as an arrow, one of the really deadly operators in terms of direction. But as he says himself, his limit is about 275 yards, which certainly doesn't make him a basket case, but it doesn't make him one of the really long rifles of the touring circuit, either.

Nicklaus, on the other hand, is one of the longest hitters the game has ever seen. Without quibbling, let us say he is capable of well over 300 yards.

Okay, put them both on a 555-yard hole, and theoretically Knudsen's 275-yard drive limit should give him a "perfect" par in five strokes. Again, theoretically, Nicklaus should be debited with a bogey if he takes five strokes to get down, because an athlete of his qualifications plays the hole "perfectly" when he uses only two strokes to get onto the green and two more to putt out.

Actually, nobody would phone the newspapers if either one of them completed this hole in four strokes, because what we think of as birdies are rather routine pars for top tournament players.

The point I am making is that "par" is a meaningless word. With the incredible improvement in the equipment and the skills of the world-class golfers over the course of the last few decades, a true par for a pro tournament is probably somewhere in the high 60s. And if the actual par is unrealistic for the pros, where does that leave us?

I think it is ridiculous for a weekend golfer to waste time worrying about what the officials have decreed "par" to be. The duffer plays his "perfect round" in the same way that the tournament pro plays his, when he tours 18 holes in the number of strokes which realistically represent his maximum skills. For instance, there may be a long, difficult par 4 which the average man may never play in regulation figures, but this should not concern him as long as he knows he has played the hole to the maximum of his ability.

However, it is vitally important for the high-scoring shooter to examine his game to determine what his maximum skill is. Heaven knows, most of us don't play anywhere near as well as we can.

I have titled this treatise *The Duffer's Guide to Bogey Golf* because I firmly believe there in nothing in the world to prohibit anyone from shooting at least that well.

And if it is true that bogey is within anyone's reach, there are certainly a lot of hackers out there playing much worse than they should be. By a recent count, there are about ten million of us in North America—men and women who actually go out to golf courses and play at least ten games a year. There are probably a few million more in the driving-range-cowboy group, for which there are no statistics. But even of the ten million golfers of record, around four million have never broken 100. Counting every club champion from the Florida Keys to the Northwest Territories, there are no more than 2,000 scratch golfers. Now do you see why I say it's an incredible feat to shoot 18 holes in par? Only one golfer in 5,000 can do it. And when Jack Nicklaus goes Down Under to an Australian tournament and shoots a 62, *ten strokes under par,* as he did in November 1971, he is simply demonstrating that he is literally one in a million.

Obviously the man who can shoot scratch must have a hell of a knack for the game. But on the other hand, the man who can shoot bogey—88 to 90—is no slouch either. Statistics show he can beat at least five million people.

Thus encouraged, let's press on and find out how to do it.

Most Duffers Act As If They Have Never Seen a Golf Course Before

Oh, I know we all yak it up on the first tee, exuding bravado from every pore. But what we are really doing is talking and thinking about everything but the problem at hand. Unfortunately, most of us start out with our minds absolutely blank, like a football team with no more game plan than, "Let's go out and really try hard."

We have completely forgotten all the tremendously valuable lessons we should have learned from the blood, sweat, and tears of our last outing.

And if we have forgotten those painful lessons, we are right back at Square One. We might as well be playing with a blindfold, because that's just about what we're doing—hiding the thinking half of your skill.

Knowing what you did wrong last time, and knowing what you did right—that's the massive Step Two toward improving your game.

That, in fact, is the big secret I was talking about.

I know it doesn't sound like much, and certainly it has nothing to do with learning how to execute the perfect stroke. But golf is not just a matter of being able to hit the ball, it's also very much a thinking game. They go together, hit and think, like ham and eggs.

Now, let's go back to that first tee. We'll assume this is your regular course. You've played it enough times so that you feel you really know it. I used to play a few courses that I thought I knew really well, until I put my knowledge to the test and found out I didn't know them at all. I knew how to get from every green onto the next tee, I knew which holes I liked and which ones scared me, I knew where the water fountains were, but I had no real idea how to actually *play* every single hole. I would get into trouble without knowing that trouble was there, or if I was aware of the danger, my mind went curiously blank and I did nothing to stay clear of it.

Let's try a test to see if you know your favorite course as well as you think you do. If you find you don't know the answers to the following questions, it's a fair bet that on any given day you are risking the possibility of adding up to 20 unnecessary strokes to your score.

1. What's the wind factor on your par 3s? On the par 4s and par 5s, at least you get another chance if you miscalculate the wind on your first shot. On par 3s, which are usually short enough so that anyone has enough distance to get on in one, setting up a birdie opportunity you get no second chance if you misread or ignore the wind. If the prevailing

breeze is usually in your face and the hole requires a 7 iron, say, you will need only an 8 or maybe even a 9 if the wind comes around behind your back and helps push your ball. The point is, you should know not only what club you normally use on a par 3, but what the wind conditions have been when the club has done the job.

2. On any par 4 or par 5 do you always know where you are? Most of us think we can gauge distance accurately by eye, but it's infinitely easier if you take the guesswork out of it. Establish at least one accurate yardage marker on each of the longer holes, by pacing it off to some fixed reference point (213 yards to the big tree, or the first trap, or the river, or whatever). Then, when your ball lands in some unfamiliar spot, as it's bound to occasionally, you can work out precisely where you are in relation to your next objective. Where this really pays off is not so much on your approach to the green, but in dealing with hazards. You should never be forced into finding yourself wondering if you have enough steam to get over a river. If you know where you are in relation to the river, it's simple: you can make it or you can't. Better to know you can't and play short, using up one stroke, than land in the water and use two.
3. On a hidden green, where is the open route to the pin? Except for the most Mickey Mouse of golf courses, there's always a wrong side from which to approach the green. If you can see the green, it's a simple matter to aim for the spot which gives you the fattest corridor for your approach. But if you can't see it, because of a dogleg or a well-placed hump, you have to remember how the green is trapped, so that even a rolling ball will stay on the grass.
4. What part does topography play on any given hole? On almost every course there are at least a couple of holes where you can effectively play the bounce, purposely aiming at a lateral hill in order to glance off it to get good position. On other holes, experience warns you to stay away from the hill because your ball is likely to roll into

big trouble. On still others, a short shot is better than a long shot in order to avoid such difficulties as downhill lies. If you can't remember from past experience how a hole should be played, you're at the mercy of the fates.

5. How much do you remember about the different greens on your course? If you are within 70 or 80 yards of the green on your approach, you're justified in attempting a pinpoint shot and going right for the cup. If you're further out, what you're usually trying to do is just land on the green, hopefully in a good position. That's hard to do if you don't remember where the good positions are in relation to where the flag might be on any given day. The average duffer usually tells himself that he will be happy with a shot that just gets him on the green—until he gets up to his ball and remembers that this particular green is 120 feet long, and by forgetting that little fact he's left himself 70 feet short.

These are only five of the basic facts you should know about your course. There are dozens more. And the more you commit to memory, the better your chances of going out and really playing the course, instead of behaving as if you'd never seen it before.

Always keep a scorecard, even if someone else offers to keep the official tally. For most duffers, the scorecard is simply a handy reference to determine who owes whom money. It shouldn't be. There's a wealth of information in that column of numbers.

Here are some of the things your card can tell you:

- *Putts.* A crack golfer expects to complete a round in 29 or 30 putts. A bogey golfer usually counts 34 to 36. If your card reveals you are averaging more than two green strokes per hole, it's telling you something. Either you don't know how to putt at all, and you'd better find out how right away, or you need a warm-up half hour on the putting clock before you set out on the course.

- *Low-scoring holes.* The Almighty is trying to tell you some thing good here. Don't ignore Him. Play the hole througl again in your mind until you can see which shot made th big difference. You'll probably find to your surprise tha it wasn't a particularly long shot; it was either smart o accurate. Keep it in mind for the next time.
- *High-scoring holes.* Rarely do we score badly on a hol because of plain bad luck. Almost always, we try some thing foolish, and we don't get away with it. Look for wha you did that was ill-advised. Remember, it's not the poo lie which gets you into trouble, it's making the shot whicl got you into the poor lie. Your scorecard is a reminder no to try that shot again.
- *Fluctuating nines.* The score going out should not be wildl different from the score going home. Course architect are devious souls, but they keep both nines fairly balanced If your scorecard is out of balance, look for the reason. If for instance, you shoot worse going out than coming home you probably need to loosen up more before the game. Tr to arrange it so you can belt a few off the practice tee withi a couple of hours of your game. If your card reveals a steady front nine and a miserable return, you may be wearing yourself out from too much pregame practicing. O you're simply out of shape and the last few holes are to much for you (a subject we'll go into later).
- *Yardage.* Get in the habit of establishing one or two distance markers in every round. Jot them down on the scorecard for transfer to a permanent notebook.

Your Score Card Is Proof: You Really Can Play Golf!

Everybody ready for the ego trip? All aboard, then. The pric of admission is at least five, and preferably ten of your ol scorecards. They are recorded proof that you can actuall shoot a lot better than you can score.

The first object of this exercise is to discover your Persona Scoring Potential.

Using myself as an example . . . I had been bumbling along, shooting 100-plus, when I decided that the century mark or worse just wasn't good enough. It was an inaccurate indicator of my game. I was pulling off too many good shots to be still pooping around in the triple numbers. So I got out all of my old scorecards and listed the best performance achieved on each of the 18 holes. (Most golf clubs have ringer competitions which perform the same function, but if you don't belong to a club—as I didn't at the time—you have to save your scorecards for this experiment.)

The cards bore out my suspicion of my Potential. If I could have stitched my composite performance into a single round, I would have come in with a 76.

Wow! Now we're talking. Seventy-six for a guy who usually soars about 30 strokes higher.

Naturally, I didn't expect to go out and shoot 76, because when my various jottings brought the details of these rounds to mind, I was able to recall that I had been a very lucky lad on quite a few of those 18 holes.

An approach shot from 20 yards out had miraculously taken a fortuitous hop and disappeared into the cup. A 67-foot putt had dropped. I was realistic enough to know I couldn't expect a repeat of shots like those.

What I could expect, though, was a repetition of those holes in which I had used my head and played according to my full capabilities. This worked out to one stroke over par on 16 holes and two strokes over par on two long and narrow holes which I personally found to be very tough. Even giving myself a pair of realistic double bogeys to shoot for, my potential for the round worked out to 90 strokes. I had shot several 99s (over ten years), so it was a solid nine strokes lower than I had ever carded before. Frankly, it seemed that I was aiming higher than my skills could produce—but damn it all, my skills *had* produced that kind of a score, in bits and pieces.

I determined that I was through with bits and pieces. I was going to put it all together.

So off I went, with my Potential Card in my pocket. Along with the list of individual hole scores, it included such additional notes as:

No. 9: Use 3 iron off tee. Driver could slice into river.

No. 14: Keep second shot well right. If in traps left, good-bye.

. . . Well, to cut the suspense, on the eighteenth hole I dropped a four-foot putt to finish the round. I then had the almost delirious pleasure of penciling in a neat 80 as my total score—19 strokes lower than any game I had ever played before!

Luck, you say? Not a bit of it. A shade spectacular, perhaps. Putts here and there stroked with the confidence that plops them into the cup. Fairway shots that stayed in play because I didn't try to rip the cover off the ball. A determination that provided me with infinitely more concentration than I could normally summon up. But all in all, quite simply a round of golf played to the maximum of my capabilities.

There is no reason why you can't have a similar experience yourself. All of us have a personal par, a set number of strokes which we *know* are all we need to get the ball off the tee and into the cup. Whenever we take more strokes than our personal par, we know they were not caused by lack of skill and ability; they were simply unnecessary strokes. When we begin to think of them that way, we gain a whole new perspective as to which precise stroke was the unnecessary one.

Once you can definitely isolate which stroke got you into trouble, you are well on your way toward never repeating it.

Once you discover your potential and begin to play to it, your game may still not be that of Lee Trevino, but it will be one hell of a sight lower than the game you normally turn in.

Some Tips on Finding Your Personal Par

Next time you go out to conquer a course, try to play it against the test of your own personal par, remembering that you are aiming not for miracles, but for realistic results.

For instance: Let us say there is a par-4, 360-yard hole, reasonably straight away, but with a river on the right and a forest on the left. You have had many an 8 or 9 on this beast because of excursions into woods and waters, but on the two or three occasions when you have kept the ball on the grass, you had no difficulty in holing out in five strokes.

Five, therefore, is your par.

If you should make it in regulation figures, as far as you're concerned it's actually a birdie.

But, you say, I can't handle a 360-yard hole in regulation figures, so don't raise my hopes.

Well, let's see.

Assuming that you can get the ball down in two putts, you will need two fairway shots averaging 180 yards each, and dead straight in both cases, to hole out in four.

Assess your game. Can you hit straight shots of 180 yards twice in a row? Most high shooters can't. But then, by playing to your own personal par, you are not trying to. All you need are three shots averaging only 120 yards each —and that you know you can make.

Forget that it's not spectacular. Forget that it's an admission that you are conceding one shot to par—because your personal par isn't four strokes, it's five.

So don't go for the groin-wrenching blast that ends all too frequently in a slice into the river, or a mis-aimed bull's-eye into the trees. Take a nice easy swing aimed for a general area which will have you in good position for the second shot—and be pleasantly surprised when your nice easy swing, delivered absolutely without tension, sails straight down the middle a gratifying 160 yards or so.

Now, here comes the iron discipline. Don't get drunk with success and attempt to pull out your heavy artillery for a boomer that will land you on the green in two. You have just accepted the probability that you can't count on slugging the pill 180 yards, so now is no time to get the enthusiastic notion that you can pull off a 200-yard effort. Instead, aim to execute another smooth stroke that will keep you on the fairway and out of trouble.

If you happen to louse up some detail, and your stroke goes only 80 yards, stay cool. After all, you have programmed this hole for three fairway strokes, and after two of them you are still playing to your own par, with a relatively easy 120-yard effort ahead of you.

On the other hand, if you played both shots right (and free from tension, you'll be amazed how many good shots you can stitch together), you are now another 160 yards along, only 40 yards from the pin.

This is your bonus for playing realistically. Only 40 yards from the pin, you have a good chance to get close enough on your approach to make a one-putt possible. Do it, and no matter how you made it, you took no more strokes on the hole than the average scratch golfer.

Make Sure You Play It One Stroke at a Time

One last tip on a point I may not have made clear.

Never, *never* stand on the first tee with no more game plan in your mind than a vague resolve to do better *on the whole game.*

You cannot take a whole round as a single unit and hope to improve on it. Each time you stand at your ball you must tell yourself that the shot you are about to make is the key stroke in the whole round. Pull this one off, and every succeeding stroke is that much easier.

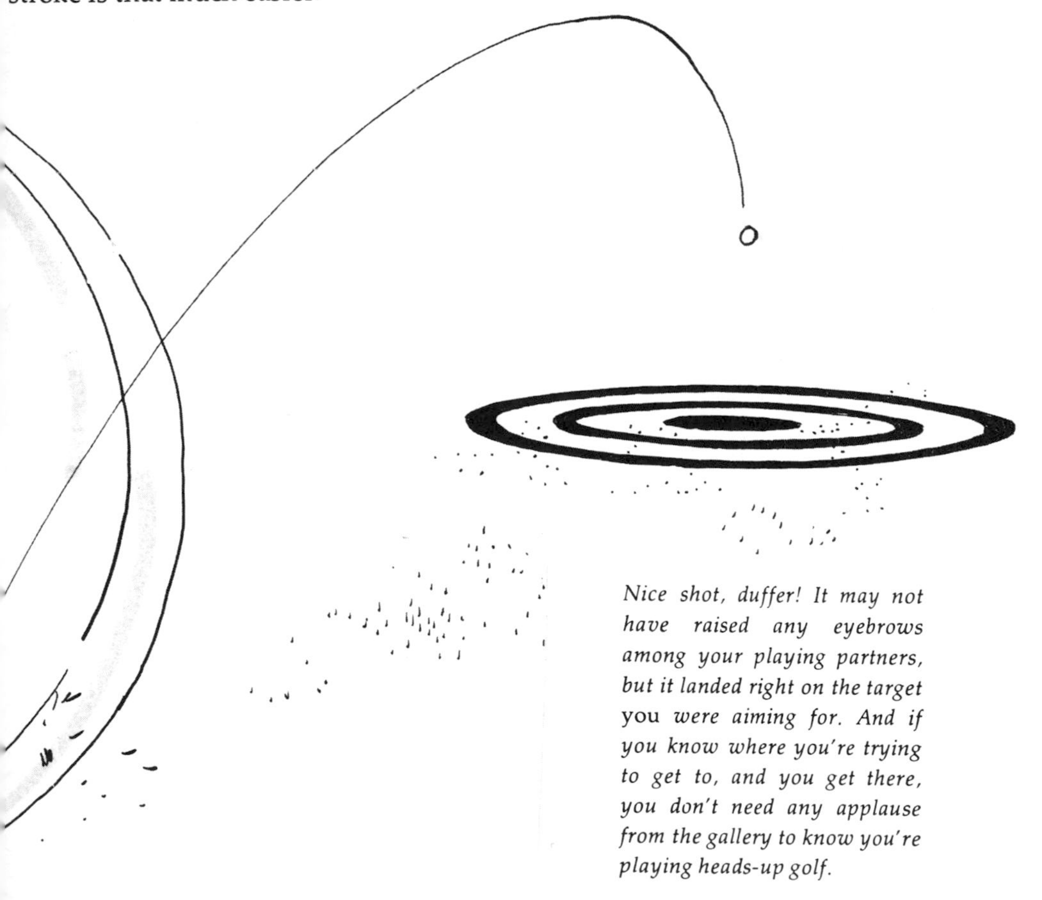

Nice shot, duffer! It may not have raised any eyebrows among your playing partners, but it landed right on the target you were aiming for. And if you know where you're trying to get to, and you get there, you don't need any applause from the gallery to know you're playing heads-up golf.

That may sound like a cliché—it may *be* a cliché—but it's more important in the long run than anything you may still have to learn about swing or stance or grip. Every stroke has a precise job to do, an ideal place to put the ball, in order to give you the very best position from which to play your next shot.

Therefore, you must take apart each hole and develop a definite plan of how you intend to play it. When you achieve the shot you tried for, it may not impress your playing partners or a passing gallery of four-year-olds, but *you* know it was a perfect shot. And that is your best insurance of playing the next one the same way.

What happens if you duff one? Doesn't that throw The Noble Experiment for a loop?

No. Not usually. What happens when you're playing good steady golf is that you win some, you lose some. Duffed shots tend to balance out with unexpectedly good shots. In any case, if it's an isolated instance—like once every second hole—forget it. You are programming yourself for bogey golf, and nine duffed shots in a round still leave you with a nine-stroke safety margin.

However, if you start running two or three duffs together, go back to Chapter One and reread it. Duffed shots are almost always errors of the brain, not of the body.

SUMMARY

1. We all shoot better than we score. Save your old scorecards and find out what your Personal Par really is—then go after it.
2. Study your course. Learn its good points and bad points as they apply to your own game.
3. Play it stroke by stroke. Always be thinking of where this shot has to go in order to make the next one easier.

4. Remember the good shots, forget the bad ones. Anger and frustration are the ruin of concentration—and you can't hit properly if you're not thinking properly.
5. Give yourself a cheery thought: By playing to your own Personal Par, even without improving your shot-making ability, you should be able to break 100—which makes you better than four million North American golfers!

Fun and Profit on the Driving Range

I think we had better start off this chapter by exploding a myth.

I admit that this may be becoming an obsession with me, but it is because I am sick to death having some guy tell me about this friend of his who can hit the ball 300 yards. Usually, it's something like this:

"All right, if you don't believe me, do you know the fourteenth hole at Happy Fantasy? Well, it's 314 yards, and I was there the day this guy landed his tee shot right on the green!"

Dreccchhhhhh ! ! ! ! !

What this guy doesn't bother to add to the story, of course, is that the markers were on the front edge of the tee, the wind was blowing at his back at about Gale Force Three, the hole was all downhill from tee to green, and the fairway was as hard-dried as a billiard table.

Duffers, if you have some Herculean friend up *your* sleeve, don't tell me about him. Just ask your club pro which of his touring colleagues can actually hit a ball, in normal conditions, and while playing a game (no driving range heroics, please) as far as you think your friend can.

The consensus of dozens of pros to whom I have put this question is that only a handful of the very best athletes in the golfing world are up in the 300-yard range.

As one pro told me, "I wish the people I teach would get it out of their heads that a drive of 250 yards—never mind 300!—is just an average stroke for a competent hitter!"

What is it, then?

"It's one hell of a good smash by a damn fine hitter!"

Well, what about all those 300-plus drives of the pros on television?

"Which pros? Nicklaus? Weiskopf? A few others? What about the other 150 guys on that tour? If they could count on a dead-straight 250 yards every time, they'd be delirious!"

What, then, is the average drive of a competent hitter?

"I'd say, given a still day and a fairway with any kind of turf on it, a good scratch golfer expects to get around 240 yards. If he goes for more, it's usually because it's a forgiving hole with plenty of fairway where he can let out the shaft and not worry if he sprays it a little. Or he may try it in a now-or-never situation—but he knows there's one hell of a risk he won't be able to keep the shot on the fairway."

Okay, you may now be asking, what is the point of all this?

Two points.

First, I think you will play much better golf if you can rid yourself of the depressing idea that there are hordes of golfers who can summon up a drive twice as long as yours whenever they stand up to the pill. The average golfer—and by that I mean the man who has some basic idea of what the golf swing is all about—should be able to expect between 180 and 200 yards out of his driver. As his game rounds into shape and he is able to sophisticate his knowledge of tempo and timing, all of his drives should sail at least 200 yards, and his better ones should occasionally go about 235.

Again, we are talking about normal conditions: little or no wind and a modern golf course fairway. Keep in mind that in professional tournaments the fairways are clipped much lower than they are for regular membership play, so that the gallery can have the vicarious thrill of watching

Regard the superman of the rubber mat. Watch him hit them to the furthest marker. Listen to him tell himself he's another Big George Bayer. But note what he fails to recognize: that the driving range fairway is as hard as a rock and will bounce and roll a ball three times the distance it will travel on golf course turf. And as far as those yardage markers—they must have been paced off by midgets. In other words, have fun at the driving range, lads—but don't take your performance too seriously.

the big sticks at work. The course superintendent has usually been instructed to cut back his rough, too, so that the pros don't get into embarrassingly deep trouble when they start spraying them a little.

As for the Sunday sluggers at the driving range—oh, boy, there is real delusion country.

I suppose I have occasionally been to a driving range which looks to have reasonably accurate yardage markers, but most of them are 10 to 20 percent on the high side. That's right: The 250-yard marker is sometimes no more than 200 to 210 yards away. And why is that? Because the driving range operators are selling entertainment. It's more fun if you think you can really hit them as far as the pros. That's why the fairway of the average driving range is bone dry and as hard as granite. A regular fairway, with the grass lush and watered, and cut to its regular height, will stop a ball in about 20 yards. A driving range will let a ball bounce and roll as much as three or four times that.

The combination of optimistic yardage markers and dried-out hard-packed fairways may give the driving range slugger the romantic idea that he can blast the ball, say, 250 yards, but if he took that exact same shot to a regular fairway he would discover that he is really poking them out about 190 yards.

And that's plenty to turn in a round of less than 90 strokes.

My second point is tied in with my last remark: for all the times you really need it to break 90, the importance of the driver is vastly overrated.

Figure it out. An average course might have three par 3s, twelve par 4s, and three par 5s, adding up to 72 strokes. This means that the duffer may take 100 whacks at the ball, but he is using the driver only 15 times. His wedge probably gets 20 workouts and his putter twice as many.

In fact, the driver wouldn't get *that* much action if the average golfer didn't automatically reach for it at almost every tee. You may have noticed, on the fourth day of a televised tournament, that the pro with the two- or three-stroke lead (whose game plan now is to just coast home without taking chances) often leaves his driver in the bag and uses instead the more reliable long irons or fairway woods.

ON WOOING THE ONE-WOOD. Try to think of your golf clubs as a harem: Love all of them, not just the driver. It's nice to be able to pound out those 250-yarders, but the No. 1 Wood is not the only club in the bag—and a dead-accurate wedge shot from 60 yards out can be pretty satisfying, too.

However, since it is the glamor weapon, and all of us lust to master it, let us take a No. 1 wood to a driving range and see what we can learn about it.

Whoops, where are you going? Not to one of those welcome mats with its permanently fixed rubber-tubing tee, I hope. If that's where you have normally been practicing, break the habit right now. Most driving ranges have a small section of grass set aside for the more serious students, and that's the place to head for.

There are several good reasons for not using mats set up on little platforms.

First, they are flat and smooth. Actual tees are not.

Second, they have seams which give you an artificial advantage when lining up to your ball and to your target. When you get onto a real course, there is no such aid and you shouldn't fall into the habit of relying on it.

Third, those permanent tees give you no practice in the proper way to tee up a ball.

Fourth, permanent tees make it too easy for you to slam out balls with machine-gun rapidity, while the ritual of reteeing after every shot is at least a slight inducement to think about what you're supposed to be doing.

Fifth, realistic iron practice is impossible using artificial tees.

So let us assume that we arrive at our patch of grass with a package of tees, our golf shoes, and a glove.

But first, we warm up.

My observation is that most people (and since most people are duffers, I guess I mean most duffers) tend to be perfunctory about loosening up. They're making a mistake. Golf is a muscle-stretching game, and if you don't get your muscles warm and loose, at best you will not be able to put your maximum power into your stroke, and at worst you can really hurt yourself.

My own method of warming up is to take out my 5 iron and go through a few gentle swings at the turf—not just swinging forward, but backward as well, like a pendulum. By swinging in both directions, I warm up my whole body, tuning it up for the necessary rhythm and balance a golf stroke requires. Only after I can feel the blood moving around all the way down through my legs and feet do I start to put any beef into these warm-up swings.

Some people prefer to work on body-stretching first, by putting the club behind their back, crooking their elbows around it, and then hip-turning as far as they can to right and left. There's a lot to be said for this exercise, too, because it starts you off right away with the reminder that a full hip-turn is a big factor in a good golf shot.

The advantage of the pendulum exercise is that, by swinging the club easily in an actual golf grip, you can work up a little sweat in the glove, softening it up, so that your left hand feels properly secure when you take your first serious cut at a ball.

As I have said, most duffers are perfunctory about the warm-up. They take a couple of ceremonial cuts at the rubber tee, then start banging out balls in gay abandon.

It may be fun, but they aren't learning much that way. My attitude is this: I want to hit every one of those 60 or 70 balls in that pail in just the way they should be hit. No excuses that I wasn't warmed up. They don't let you have ten or eleven mulligans when you step up to an actual golf tee, and you shouldn't think in those terms at the practice range either. As much as possible, you should be trying to duplicate actual playing conditions.

Otherwise, you are simply amusing yourself by swinging a golf club, with nothing at stake and no real interest in the results. The game of golf and the recreational activity of bashing out a few helter-skelter balls are quite different occupations, and should not be confused.

Put another way: just hitting the ball is the easy part; making it do what it is supposed to do, go where it is supposed to go, that is golf.

Don't misunderstand me, though. There's absolutely nothing wrong with spending an hour or so at a practice range batting out a few dozen balls. It's fun. And it's great therapy, too. It gets rid of all kinds of tensions and hostilities. Look at all those white-shirt-and-tie types you see on the ranges any noon hour. You think they're seriously practicing golf? Uh-uh.

"Take *that*, Mr. Shlockmyer!"

That's what they're saying.

However, if you arrive at the practice tee with the serious intent of improving your game, here are several programs to choose from:

1. Single Club Practice.

   The two hardest clubs for me to master are the No. 1 wood and the No. 1 iron. Whenever I determine to work on them, I force myself to concentrate on their distinctive characteristics by taking one or the other to the range and leaving all my other clubs at home. (If I bring everything, I'll use everything, and the problem clubs will get only passing attention.) Then I work on the problem in the following order: (1) Development of a comfortable swing. No matter where the ball goes, good or bad, if the swing doesn't feel right with a problem club, you still have problems. It might be anything: improper address, overcompensating grip, stance, swing, and so on. Only when it begins to feel comfortable do I start looking where the ball is going. (2) The flight of the ball. If I am comfortable and making good contact, and yet the ball is still taking a 9-iron flight with a 1-iron stroke, I stay with this aspect of the problem until I get the flight to flatten out to the proper trajectory. (3) Direction. Once it feels right, and once its trajectory looks right, I work on threading the needle. (4) Distance always comes last. If everything else is in hand, distance is only a matter of increasing power while maintaining finesse.

2. Distance by Numbers.
   I know all kinds of high-scoring players who take a full bag of clubs to the course, then use only two or three of them. They don't trust the others. Eventually, they come to rely on two or three clubs so heavily they will use, say, a 5 iron to perform the duties of every club from the 3 wood to the 7 iron. This practice program helps break that habit: Start with the 9 iron and make a mental note of where the ball lands on its first bounce. The roll doesn't count. Then take the 8 iron (or 7 iron, if you have one of those 3-5-7-9 sets) and, using the same swing, aim to have the ball land a few yards further along. The 7 iron goes a little further, and so on. The idea is to take each club in sequence and progressively extend your yardage, *letting the club do the work*. Don't try to push any of the shots. Get used to the idea that the 5 iron (or whatever) is *not* an all-purpose club—and that a 4-iron shot goes further than a 6-iron shot because of club engineering and not because it is hit harder. If you duff a shot, start all over again at the 9 iron, the object being to run through all of your clubs in sequence and make them do what they're supposed to do. Note the average distance between strokes. With most people it's about ten yards more per club; with some people it's as little as five yards. Knowing your own "spacing" is important.
3. Simulated Game Practice.
   This can be a sobering exercise for the man who has batted out a couple of good ones and then mentally projects them into 50 good ones and sees himself breaking par. All you do is play your own course on the driving range. Take your tee shot, estimate where it lands in relation to where that would put you on your own course, then make your next shot as if you were really on your home fairway. When you estimate that your shots have brought you to an approach position, aim for a precise spot on the range grass. If

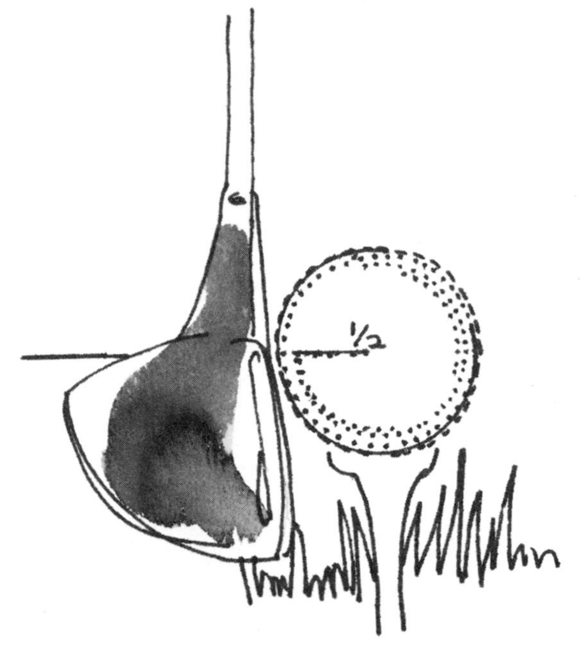

The correct tee height for the beginner: About half the ball should be above the clubhead when the driver is soled behind it.

your ball lands within ten yards (no matter where it may bounce and roll), assume you're on the green, count an automatic two putts, and go on to the next hole. One concession: all fairway shots can be set up on a good piece of grass, but no using tees except for tee shots. One prohibition: if you flub a shot, it counts. Frankly, this game drives me nuts because I find it difficult to concentrate; that's why it's good exercise—discipline.

4. Bad Luck Practice.

With my luck, even if I were playing on Astro Turf, my ball would land right on a zipper. Still, you have to learn to play the bad lies sooner or later, and this is an excellent practice to give you confidence. Using any fairway club you wish, drop a ball on the grass and take your shot without improving your lie. All you have to remember is that poor lies usually look a lot worse than they really are. If you hit down and carry through (we'll go into this in detail later on), you'll find no trouble with 95 percent of them. In fact, sometimes a poor lie leads to a very good shot because you concentrate harder on being precise. On the other hand, whenever the rules permit, use a tee. A poor lie makes most beginners and high-scoring shooters uncomfortable, and at this point in your improvement program you need all the confidence and freedom from tension you can get. For every shot within your present range of skills—whether using driver or wedge, whether into the wind or with it—tee the ball fairly high, so that approximately one-half of it is above the driver when the club is soled firmly behind the ball. Then, for insurance, tamp down the turf behind the ball so there's nothing to deflect the clubhead on its way toward impact.

SUMMARY

1. As a primary objective, aim to develop a consistently straight drive which sacrifices distance for direction. Anyone who can drive 180 yards will increase through practice to 235 or so, which is more than enough.
2. Always warm up before either play or practice. You can hurt yourself if you don't.
3. On the driving range, practice on the grassy section, not on the fixed tees. Artificial conditions don't really help you to improve.
4. Don't be deluded by driving range yardage markers. Your goal is to hit the ball properly and to hit it straight; distance is only a distraction.
5. Have a game plan in mind when you visit the driving range. Try to arrive with a precise problem and leave with it solved.
6. Run through the clubs in sequence and learn for yourself that the difference in flight and distance is obtained through proper club selection, and not through trying to hit the ball harder.
7. Through practice, develop confidence that good shots are still possible from poor lies.
8. Remember the correct tee height: half the ball showing above the clubhead when the driver is soled directly behind it.

Straight Shooting Made Easy

Generally speaking, there are only two basic causes of a really bad shot. One is a breakdown in the swing, and the other is a basic defect in the grip. We'll get to the swing in Chapter Six. Right now, let's concentrate on the grip.

Is there anyone out there at the back of the class who doesn't know how to grip a golf club.

It would be interesting, if this were a classroom, to see if anybody raised their hands. Most of us, after we have been playing for a while, are curiously defensive about our grip. "For goodness' sake, don't ask me to change the way I hold the club, that's the only thing I know I can do right!"

If that's so, if you really do have a good grip, then someone must have taught it to you, or you are a very remarkable fellow. Because the proper way to grip a golf club is just about diametrically opposite from the way in which you'd grip anything else of the same general size and shape, such as an axe or a baseball bat or a piece of rope or a hammer.

Surprised? Dubious? So was I. And stubborn enough to waste about 5,000 golf shots holding the club the wrong way. Let's see if we can save you from a similar waste of time.

People with small hands usually find that the eight-finger grip gives them the most control: none of the fingers overlap; they're all in a row down the shaft, and all eight fingers come in contact with the club.

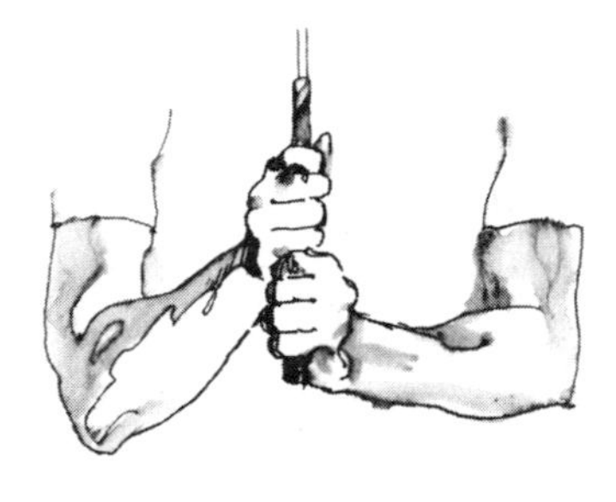

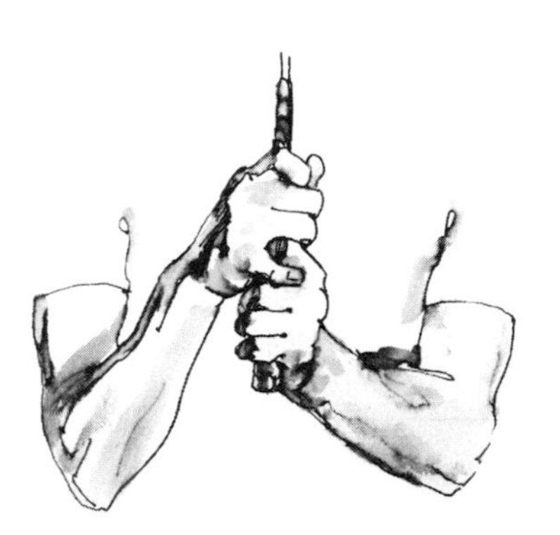

In the left-hand illustration, all eight fingers grip the club; a good grip for players with small hands. Next is the Vardon Grip, which is best for the average golfer. Here the pinky finger of the right hand lies in the groove of the first and second fingers of the left hand. Right-hand illustration: Looking down at your hands, you should be able to see the V of the thumb and forefinger pointing generally toward the right shoulder. Note that there's no break in the wrists.

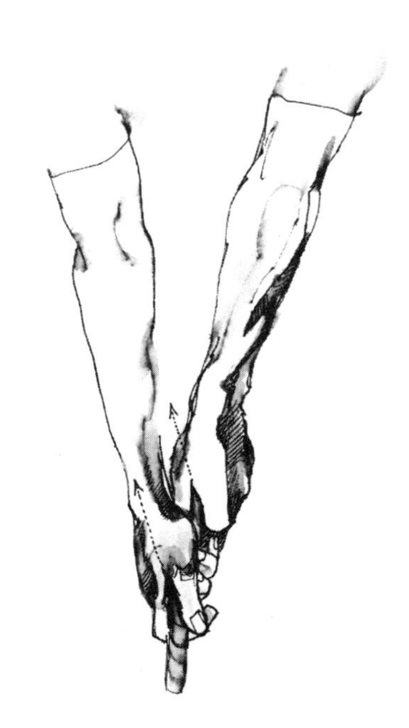

The rest of us, that is, the overwhelming majority, are best suited to what is known as the Harry Vardon grip, in which the pinky of the right hand overlaps the first and second fingers of the left hand. It does not touch the club at all, but rests in the groove formed by those two fingers.

This may seem a little confusing, but the stray finger finds its position quite naturally as long as you remember that the third or ring finger of the right hand lays right against the first finger of the left hand. Squeezed out of the play, so to speak, there's no place else for the right pinky to go. Don't try to jam it between these fingers so that it grips the club (this is known as the interlocking grip), because if it finds a way to touch the club it will grab onto it—and that's not its function.

Here is the important point: even though your hands have eight fingers, two thumbs, and two palms, only five fingers and the pad of flesh in the immediate palm behind them are involved in gripping the club. Nothing else. All the rest of your manual equipment is strictly along for the ride.

The grippers are the last three fingers of the left hand and the middle two fingers of the right hand.

This boggles the minds of most beginners. Everything in their experience tells them that they should be holding onto the shaft with everything at their command. I think the reason for this is the beginner's not unnatural belief that you have to hold the club hard in order to hit the ball hard in order to make it go far. Not so. The golf club does not function at its best as a sheer power weapon. I will explain this in detail later, but for the moment let us concentrate simply on how to hold the club.

The best way to get the idea of a proper grip is to start off without holding the club at all. Just stand up, feet about shoulder width apart, and put your palms together in front of you as if you were praying. Now straighten your elbows and extend your arms in front of you, hands still pressed

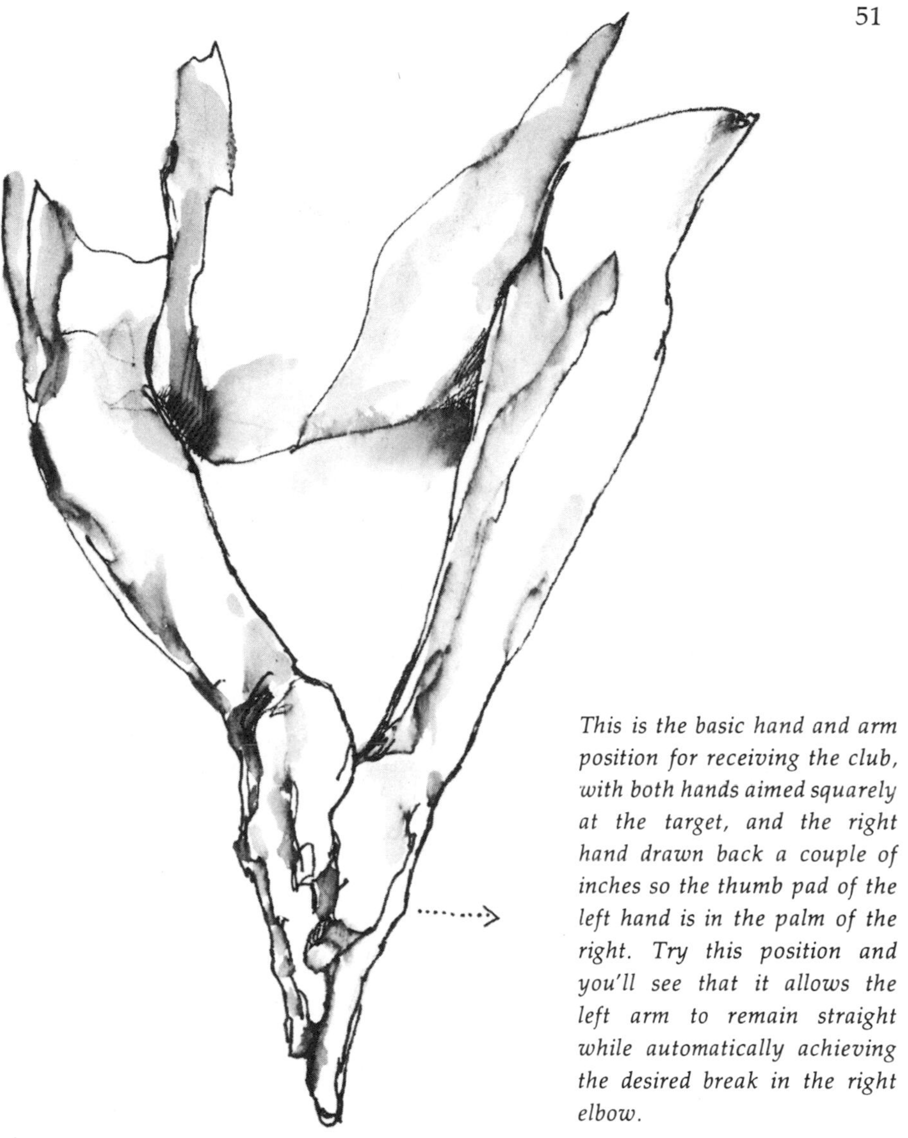

This is the basic hand and arm position for receiving the club, with both hands aimed squarely at the target, and the right hand drawn back a couple of inches so the thumb pad of the left hand is in the palm of the right. Try this position and you'll see that it allows the left arm to remain straight while automatically achieving the desired break in the right elbow.

together, with your arms at the angle they would normally assume if you were actually holding a golf club. When you get to that position, let your right shoulder drop slightly so that your right hand slips down a couple of inches into the palm of the left hand.

Now look at your hands.

Both of them are in precisely the right position to hit a golf ball dead straight. That is to say, the back of the left hand and the palm of the right hand are pointed straight at the target.

The trick now is to stick a golf club between them without disturbing this perfect hand alignment.

There are probably all kinds of grips which will allow this perfect hand alignment to be maintained as long as you remain motionless in the position of address. But there is only one grip in which the alignment can be maintained throughout the entire golf swing.

That is when the club is gripped with *only* the last three fingers of the left hand and the middle two fingers of the right hand.

With any other grip—such as slipping the shaft into the palms of the hands and really getting a fistful of stick, or pinching the shaft between the thumb and fingers as if you're holding a carving knife and fork—the perfect hand alignment is destroyed the instant you start into the backswing, and only a fluke will bring it back in time to produce a straight shot.

Never settle for a grip simply because it feels comfortable at address, because neither you nor the club will be in that position when you actually hit the ball. Everybody forgets this. We all fall into the habit of trying to feel some sense of future power at the moment of address, overlooking completely the fact that, at the real moment of power, the hands and feet and hips and club and everything else *are* somewhere else.

Back to the grip. Let's try it for real.

Place the sole of your driver flat on the ground, with the face square to the target. Do not tilt it up and toe it in, a device which many duffers adopt in the vain hope that it will cure them of slicing. It won't. Now bring back the shaft so that the top of the grip rests on the inside of the upper left thigh. The club is now in the correct position to receive your grip. If you're trying this with an iron rather than the driver (which has that big fat sole to tell you where "flat on the ground" is) make sure that you line the bottom edge of the clubface square to the target. If you line up the top edge, you'll be toeing in again.

Settle the underside of the shaft into the crease between the palm and the last three fingers of your left hand. Take a firm grip with these fingers, keeping the first finger and thumb totally relaxed.

Now fit the middle two fingers of the right hand under the shaft so that right ring finger and left first finger are touching. If you pull the right hand snugly against the left, the "floating pinky" should rest comfortably in its proper position. Because the pinky is not part of the grip, the shaft will settle not quite so deeply into the crease between the right fingers and palm; the underside of the shaft will rest more on the pad of the first knuckle. Open your hands a little and you should be able to see clearly the snug fit of the shaft in the five-finger vise.

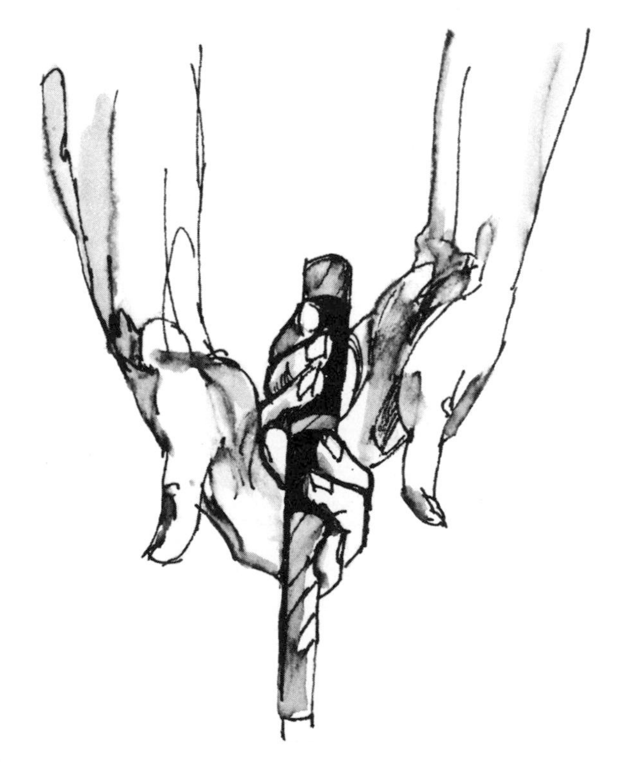

Only five fingers do any real work in holding the club, the last three fingers of the left hand and the middle two of the right hand. Even though the thumbs and forefingers should be settled comfortably on the shaft, the beginner should think of them as merely being along for the ride.

Now close the left hand so that the left thumb rests comfortably and naturally on top of the shaft, slightly to the right of center. Finally, close the right hand over the left so that the left thumb tucks nearly into the pad of the right palm. Remember, the thumb and forefinger of the right hand do not take an active part in gripping the club. Keep them relaxed.

Look at your hands again.

1. You should be able to see just a peep of the first two knuckles of the left hand, and very little more.
2. The crease between the thumb and forefinger of each hand, known as the V, should point in the general direction of the right shoulder.
3. Most important—and to be achieved at the expense of numbers 1 and 2—the backs of the hands should still be pointed dead at the target.

Don't try to become a contortionist to achieve perfection in the first two points above. Everyone's hands are different, and yours may not allow you to get into the classic position. The big thing is number 3, keep the backs of the hands square to the target.

As for the the nongripping fingers and thumbs, let's say it once more: keep them relaxed. Wherever they settle comfortably is where they should be. They can touch the shaft if you wish, as long as you don't try to grip with them, or they can just flop around in the breeze, as long as they don't get in the way.

The next point is kind of tricky. It concerns " the break in the wrist," which is not the same thing as "the cocking of the wrists," and I had better explain the difference between the two right now.

Place your hand and forearm flat on a table, palm down. Keeping the forearm motionless, slide the palm back and forth across the table surface without lifting it. Once you have the motion, do it with your fist closed. That is the basic action of "cocking the wrist," more or less a lateral movement.

Now take the same position again, hand open and palm down, and instead of making a lateral movement, lift the hand up and down while the forearm remains motionless. Try it with the closed fist. That action is known as "breaking the wrist."

Breaking the wrist is very definitely a no-no insofar as a proper grip is concerned. Here's why. Take the club in your hand and break your wrists. Instantly all four knuckles of the left hand come into view, because the left hand has to come up on top of the shaft. Same thing with the right hand.

Even worse—potentially disastrous, in fact—the backs of the hands are no longer pointed anywhere near the target. They're aiming toward the sky.

When the wrist is unbroken, you should be able to achieve a straight unbroken line all the way from your left shoulder through the left elbow and wrist to the back of the hand. In order to do this, unless you're multi-jointed, the inside of the left elbow should not be pointing toward your body, it should be facing straight out in front of you. This out-turning of the elbow tends to lock the whole left arm in a straight line. And that's how it's supposed to be.

The right arm follows a slightly different configuration. Although the right hand is lower down the shaft than the left, the right arm doesn't s-t-r-e-t-c-h to get it there. Instead, the right shoulder just drops a little. There is also a little break in the right elbow, so that the inside of the right elbow does not face straight out in front of you; it cants in slightly toward the body. The reason for the right-elbow-break is that when you go into the backswing with the left arm straight, the right elbow acts as the pivot of that whole motion. The elbow breaks slightly at address to eliminate any jerkiness during this pivoting maneuver.

Again, this is a point we'll discuss fully later. The point

to remember now is to keep the right wrist in as unbroken a line as possible, with the back of the hand pointing straight at the target. If the right hand is allowed to slide under the shaft, so that the back of the hand is beginning to point toward the ground . . . do you know what's happening? That right hand is secretly preparing to take over the swing the instant you start to pull the clubhead back from the ball.

Resist like crazy any urge you may have to get a good strong grip on the club with the right hand.

Conversely, work to develop the firmest possible left-hand grip.

Here's why.

The left hand will never try to hit the ball. That's not its function. The function of the whole left side—hand, arm, shoulder, hip, toenails, everything—is to control the club and control the swing all the way up into the top of the backswing and all the way down again until the last few inches before the clubface meets the ball.

It is in this last 12 inches, known as the impact area, that the right hand gets its chance to do its stuff. What happens is that the wrists uncock with a snap, and the whole power of the driving right side is poured into the hand, enabling it to lash into the back of the ball. This is not because the right hand is stronger than the left, either. It's because of that right elbow I mentioned earlier. It has been bent throughout the swing, while the left elbow has been kept straight. In the last split second the right elbow and right wrist straighten briskly into the shot, and it is this crack-the-whip action which supplies the real power.

But remember this: If the right hand is allowed to take any important part in the proceedings before its appointed time, you will *not* achieve full power and you will not hit the ball straight.

I think it was Tommy Armour who said that the left hand guides the club into the ball so that the right hand can smash the hell out of it.

The trouble is, the right hand wants to get into the act too early. Instead of performing their proper function in their proper sequence, the hands get into a war with each other and the right hand wins—and takes over completely. Released from the confines of a proper grip—that is, given too strong a position too early—the right hand simply jerks the clubhead off the grass willy-nilly, whips it away up into the air over the golfer's head, then brings it down in a graceless, clubbing motion. The path of the clubhead follows a route which is infamously known as "outside-in," and the clubface doesn't really smash into the ball at all. It swipes at it.

And when that happens, you slice.

Some duffers who really try to murder the ball with an excessive right hand have been known to develop a slice so vicious they can almost make their shot land behind them. If you're one of them, take heart. I guarantee I can eliminate your slice if you follow the *Guide* with diligence.

We do not get into the full intricacies of the swing until a later chapter, but since the subject has been touched on here is how the proper grip affects the proper swing.

As I have said, the overpowering grip of the right hand has a tendency to lift the club off the grass too quickly. But when the left hand maintains it control, with the left elbow turned out and the back of the hand vertical and square to the target—there is no way the left hand can comfortably lift the clubhead off the grass. Our joints just don't work that way.

The whole left side is locked into a position in which the left hand can get the clubhead moving only by *shoving it back* rather than lifting it up. Thus, in order to get any kind of a backswing at all, the left arm and shoulder are forced to follow the hand as one whole integrated unit—which is exactly its proper function. Nothing breaks down, nothing comes apart. The whole left side turns into the backswing around the pivot of the bent right elbow, and the club is forced to travel around and behind the golfer's shoulders—and not up and over his head.

On the way back down, the firm left side reverses the motion and the clubhead follows the same flight path that it described on the way up. The result is that the face of the club comes in nice and low along the grass, hits the back of the ball squarely, and continues on an "inside-out" path toward the target.

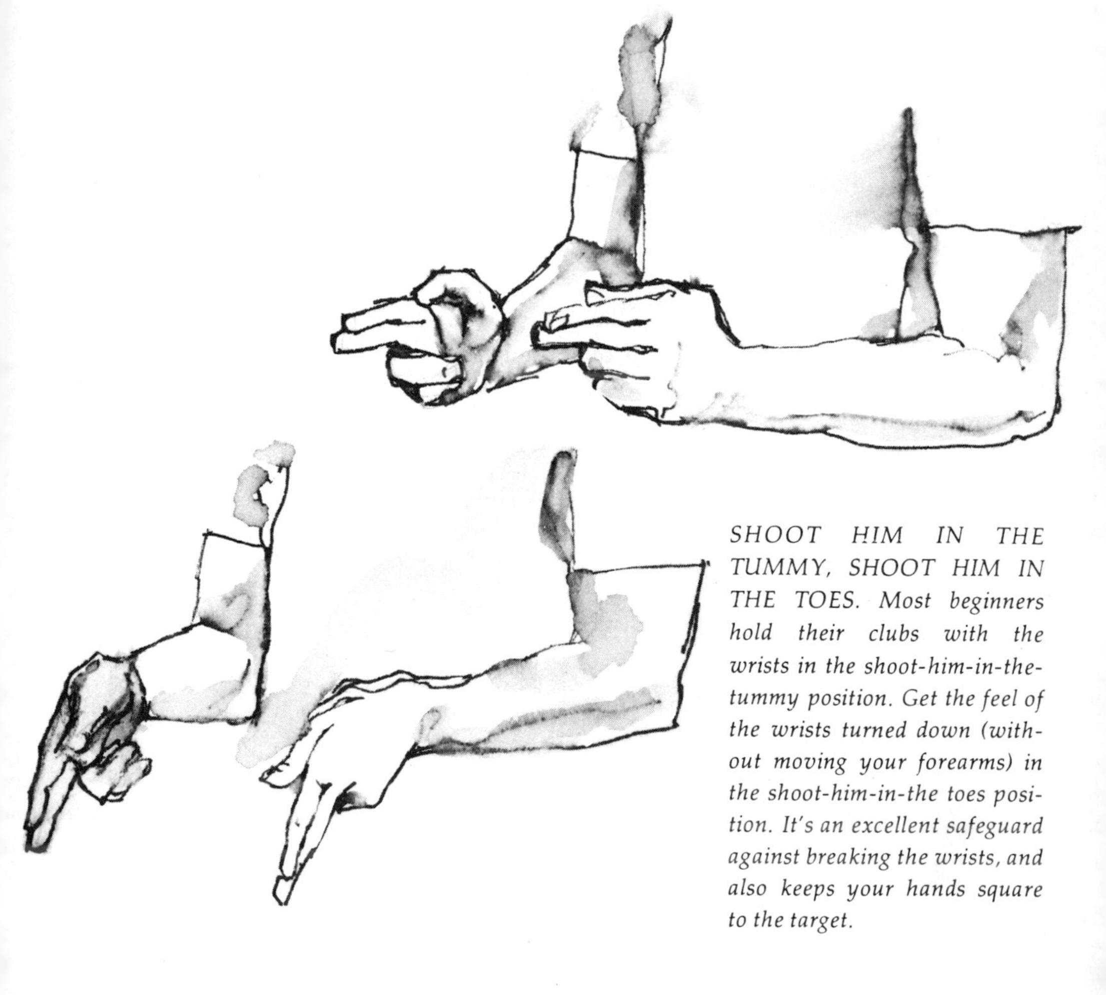

SHOOT HIM IN THE TUMMY, SHOOT HIM IN THE TOES. Most beginners hold their clubs with the wrists in the shoot-him-in-the-tummy position. Get the feel of the wrists turned down (without moving your forearms) in the shoot-him-in-the toes position. It's an excellent safeguard against breaking the wrists, and also keeps your hands square to the target.

It's a simple matter: get it started out in the right direction, don't let the swing fall apart by breaking the left elbow, and it has to return the same way. Arnold Palmer is so sure that this is the big secret that he says the only part of the swing you have to worry about is the first 12 inches of the backswing. If you can start it off low along the grass, you've got it made.

A final check on proper grip:

I have had some difficulty in coming up with just the right way to describe the vertical position of the hands, and I know this is going to seem a little silly, but it does get the point across. Imagine you are holding two six guns, pointing right at the bad guy's belly button. Then you change your mind and decide to shoot into the ground at his feet. Using your wrists only, tilt the guns down.

That turned-down wrist position is exactly the right wrist angle for a proper golf grip. (Who says TV westerns aren't educational?)

Only one last point remains: How tightly do you hold onto the club?

I have tried every degree of firmness and have come up with the following measure: The left-hand grip must be firm enough to be able to solidly control the club when it is lifted by the left hand only. The right hand is allowed to grip the club firmly only to establish that my fingers are in the right place and comfortable, then I slack off to the point where I can feel that I am holding the club more with the left hand than the right. This ensures that the left hand is holding the club strongly enough to maintain control of it all through the swing, and the right hand is holding it lightly enough that it will not overpower the left hand too early.

In any case, never take a death grip on the club. In the golf swing, smoothness is everything, and it's difficult to remain smooth and fluid if you're tensed up.

Actually, it won't take you very long to find out if you're too weak or too strong in your grip. The pain in your hands will let you know. Too firm a grip leads to callouses; too slack, to blisters. If the grip is super-slack, the shaft will turn in your hands and you will achieve a really swell mis-hit—which is doubly painful because you will probably be watching another $1.50 disappearing into the boondocks.

SUMMARY

1. Only five fingers grip the club: the last three fingers of the left hand and the middle two fingers of the right. Everything else is along for the ride.
2. If your grip is correct, you should be able to see no more than a peeping view of the first knuckles of the left hand; the Vs of your forefingers and thumbs should point toward your right shoulder; and the backs of both hands must point straight to the target.
3. The left elbow is straight, inside of the elbow pointing out; the right elbow is slightly bent, inside of the elbow canting slightly in toward the middle of the body.
4. Don't worry if any of the positions described feel at first to be a little awkward or uncomfortable when you stand at address. What's important is that it will feel right at the moment of impact.
5. Remember, you control the swing with the left hand, you hit the ball with the right—in that order.
6. Always think in terms of a grip which allows you to start the backswing by shoving the clubhead backward, low, along the grass. Do not allow a grip which permits you—in fact, invites you—to lift the clubhead straight up and over your head.
7. At address, keep both wrists turned down (firing at his feet), to minimize any tendency to either break the straight line from shoulder to back of hand, or to cock the wrists prematurely.

The Stance: Where and How to Find It

In this chapter we will cover both where and how to stand, a facet of the game in which most duffers get off on the wrong foot. In fact, it is the rare 100-plus shooter who has any idea what his feet are supposed to be doing. Except in such rare cases as need not immediately concern us—such as when the ball is nestling in the crotch of a tree—the ball is always played somewhere between the feet.

Ho, ho, you say, who doesn't know that?

Maybe you know it, but take a look at your ball and foot placement next time you're out, and see whether what you know has any bearing on what you actually do. It is not unusual for a duffer to know in his head what he should be doing, yet have failed to send the good word down to his physical parts.

Both the grip and the stance have undergone some second thoughts in recent years. I think most experts today opt for the Vardon overlapping grip, but there is still a strong division when it comes to stance. I'll explain the two major techniques and you can take your pick.

The traditional technique decrees that one play the ball toward the left foot for distance, and toward the right foot for accuracy. Shots demanding a combination of distance and accuracy are played squarely between the feet. In other words, when you're using the driver, the ball is played an

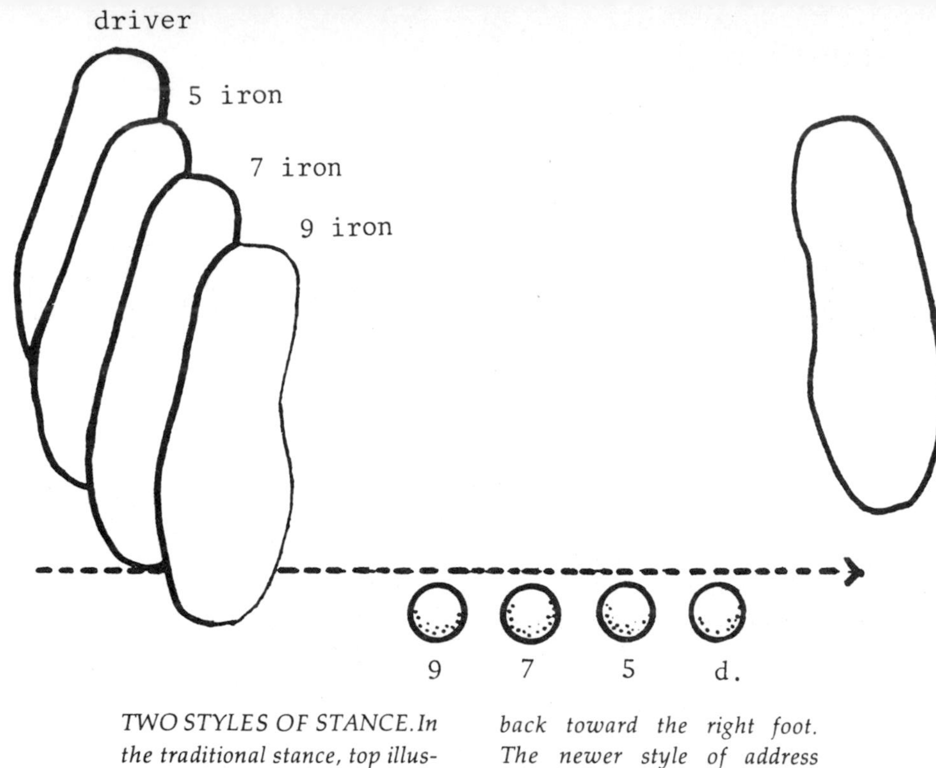

TWO STYLES OF STANCE. In the traditional stance, top illustration, the right foot is drawn back from the line of flight and the ball is played off the left heel. As we go up the clubs. we come in closer, eventually drawing the right foot over the line of flight in the Open Position. The ball position inches back toward the right foot. The newer style of address keeps the ball off the left heel for almost all shots, both feet remain parallel to the line of flight, and the right foot inches in slightly only if the golfer feels more comfortable with a tighter stance for those short precision shots.

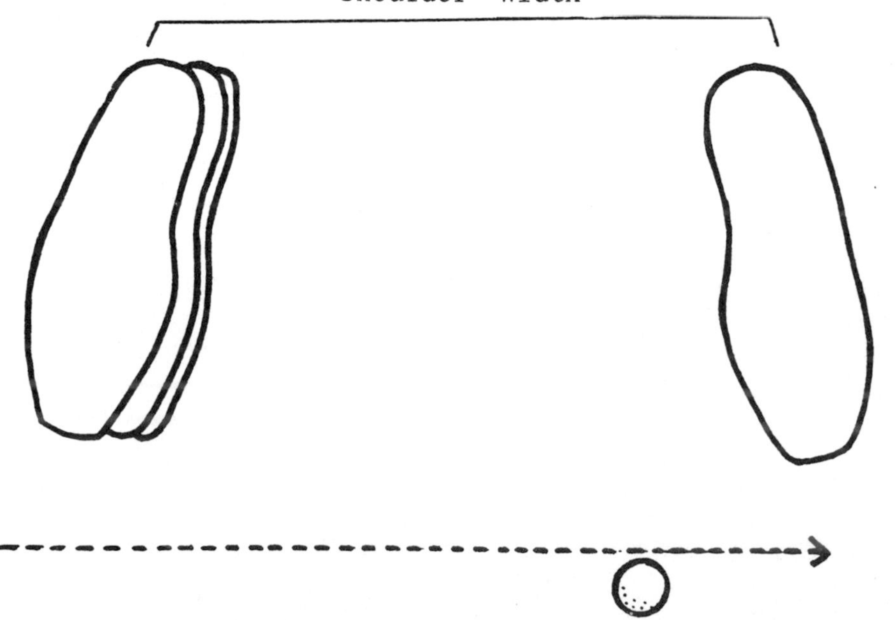

inch or two back of the left heel. When you're going dead for the stick with the 9 iron or wedge, it is played almost as far back as the right heel. Fairway irons call for the ball to be just about in the middle. When I played this way, the center-line club for me was the 4 iron. I played the ball an inch or so forward of center for the 3 iron, and an inch or so back toward the right heel with the 5 iron.

In all cases the weight is evenly distributed between the feet, but with the fore-and-aft distribution definitely favoring the heels over the toes.

Coupled with this rule regarding the placement of the ball vis-à-vis the feet is a further refinement regarding the placement of the feet vis-à-vis the target. Thus we have the open and the closed positions. In the open position your body tends to face the target, with your left foot back and your right foot forward. The closed position reverses the feet so that your body points slightly away from the target. The square position, of course, is that in which you line up your feet so that the body is parallel to the target.

Most teachers who favor the traditional method tell their pupils that shots using the clubs from the 5 iron up to the 3 wood require a generally square stance. The driver is used from a closed position in which the left foot is shoved a little bit over the intended line of flight. With the higher-lofted clubs—from the 6 to the wedge—it is the right foot which is placed over the line, thus opening your body to the target. The foot slides forward about an inch with the 6, and up to six inches with the wedge.

The reason for all these minute alterations of foot and ball placement is to allow you to take exactly the same swing with every club and yet be able to meet the ball each time with a perfectly square-to-the-target clubface. In other words, the minute adjustments of the body compensate for the differences in the length of shaft and the variation of loft in the face of the clubs.

If you do everything properly, there is not a thing wrong with this technique. Much better golfers than you and I will ever be have used it with championship-winning results. But to my mind, that's the trouble with it: It demands better golfing skills than most duffers have going for them. All that switching around tends to confuse the beginner. When he should be bearing down on the smoothness of the swing, he is still using a little bit of his mind to fret about his feet.

The more recently developed style of stance requires no great feat of memory. All you have to learn is one position:

Every shot is played off the left heel.

Every shot is played from the square stance.

You simply line yourself up with the ball off the heel by an inch or two, make sure your feet are parallel to the line of flight you want the ball to take, and that's all there is to it.

But not quite.

That's it, duffer! Sway back off balance so you can get a real good lick at the ball—but don't blame me if you don't come within a foot of it.

In order for all the factors of the swing to come together properly, the weight must always tend toward the left foot rather than the right.

If you think about it a bit, the reason for the weight placement is common sense. There is always a danger that you are going to sway in every swing. The action of the backswing, for instance, is a very strong physical motivation to sway back into the swing, like a pitcher rearing back to deliver a fast ball. Your hands and arms and shoulders are going back, why not let the body follow?

Uh-uh. Do that, and here's what happens. There's the ball, someplace up front off the left heel, and here's your body, someplace back over the right foot—and as they used to say in the old vaudeville joke, you can't get there from here!

The danger of putting the weight on the right foot is that it allows even a little backward sway to become accentuated, because you are using the foot to balance on.

Even if you do manage to hit the ball, you'll probably top it because you can't quite reach it squarely. The necessity is not merely to reach the ball, but to come into and through it. With the weight directly over the ball, you are able to keep hitting through well past the moment of impact.

Mind you, if you watch closely you'll see the odd top pro rearing back, lifting his left foot off the ground, trying to get the very last millimeter of extension into his windup . . . but, brother, that top pro knows exactly what he is doing, and he has disciplined his body to function properly even at the outer limits of balance.

While we're on this topic, you may be thinking that you have seen some very able golfers get off fine shots without apparently following any of the rules I have been describing. That's so. It's the prerogative of experts in any field of endeavor. But the beginner has to start with a fairly rigid set of Do's and Don'ts, from which he deviates only after he becomes expert, or because physical limitations demand it.

Therefore, you may consider my suggestions regarding stance and ball position and weight distribution as the starting point from which you are free to make the minor variations your own physique may require.

You may find, for instance, that you just can't get your left hip out of the way in time if you take a perfectly square stance, and that you have to open your stance a little for every shot. Fine. Go ahead. Do it that way.

Most wedge shots are played from a more open stance, even among golfers who generally accept the rules I have just outlined. The reason for this is that when you are looking for only 20 or 30 yards, the shot is played almost totally with the arms and not with the body; the good golfer likes to get his left hip out of the way first, so that he doesn't get the feeling that it is blocking the freedom of movement of his wrists and arms.

He may also opt to play the ball toward his right foot for short shots because he wants the face of the wedge to go under the ball (this is no place to top the shot), and he is not in much danger of body sway since he is only using his arms and hands.

In every case, though, the weight *must* be back on the heels. If you allow yourself to fall into the habit of getting your weight tilted over onto your toes, you are giving yourself the extra handicap of trying to hit while off balance. It never works.

Let's press on to the width of the stance and the attitude of the feet.

Here again, the rules are basic. Once you have them fixed in your mind, please feel free to experiment. When you take your stance, what you are looking for is a positioning of the body which allows you to remain comfortable throughout the swing, maintaining your balance while being able to take a full cut at the ball.

Generally, your feet should be shoulder width apart and your toes should turn slightly outward. I think all the good players keep the left foot open—the toe slightly out-turned—but some like to keep the right foot square, so that they have a good firm launching pad to drive into the shot.

It's a matter really of giving up one thing to achieve another. If you square off the rear foot, there's no doubt that you can drive harder into the shot than if it's turned slightly away from the target. But the more you square away the right foot, the more difficult it is to get a really full backswing. The right foot inhibits a complete hip-turn.

As for distance between the feet, most beginners err on the wide side.

They have this idea that they must get themselves solidly planted so they can really murder the ball. In fact, just the opposite happens. The wider the stance, the more difficult it is to execute a full backswing, because the hips lock too early.

However, you'll remember that I did say earlier that golf is a game of contradictions. Look at Doug Sanders, the runner-up to Jack Nicklaus in the 1970 British Open. He's famous for his extremely wide stance and a swing which is so abbreviated that, as someone once cracked, "It looks as if he's swinging in a telephone booth." Yet, he can bat the ball a mile.

Or better still, look at yourself. If you're using a wide stance and you're not meeting the ball with authority, close up to shoulder width apart and give it a try.

One verity on which all good golfers agree is that you must never stand up to the ball stiff-legged, with your knees locked in the straight-line position. This is almost certainly going to make you lean forward, putting your weight on your toes.

When you take your position at address, put your weight

onto your heels and then let your knees buckle slightly, as if you were about to sit down and then suddenly stopped. This should lower your behind a couple of inches closer to the ground. Caution: don't try to achieve this lowering of the body simply by stooping over. The back should be absolutely straight, the rump should stick out slightly, and the knees should be bent slightly.

Please reread the above paragraph. Its instruction is extremely important. If you do *not* sag at the knees, it is very difficult to start into the backswing smoothly, it is impossible to take a full backswing because of the restriction of the locked knees, and the lifting motion of the backswing leaves the extended body with no alternative but to lift the left foot off the ground. The couple of inches of sag is "the slack which permits the lift to happen without pulling your foot off the grass.

THE PROPER STANCE. Back straight, knees flexed, weight well back on the heels. And don't be afraid to stick your rear end out; it's a great help in forcing you to bring your whole body weight directly over your feet, in perfect balance.

The Target Is Out There Somewhere

Most duffers have only the haziest awareness that the stance has two duties to perform. As I hope the previous section has made clear, it puts you in the right position to hit the ball properly; but its equally important function, of course, is to put you in the right position to hit the target.

As Arnold Palmer has said, "I can cut the score of the average golfer by ten strokes if I could simply club him and *point him in the right direction.*"

When you are in the early stages of your golfing skills—which is to say, hardly skilled at all—it seems impossibly difficult to make the ball go anywhere near the general direction in which you want it to go. You spend half your time stalking through the woods trying to find out where the hell the thing has gone. Then you watch an expert booming those 200-yard iron shots tight to the stick, and secretly you can't put down the notion that those were lucky strokes, that nobody can actually aim a golf shot that precisely.

But watch any top golfer on the practice tee. He'll send a kid a couple of hundred yards down the fairway to shag his balls, then drop them one after another, literally at the kid's feet. Plop, plop, plop. It drives you green with envy.

Agreed, most of the duffer's problem is involved in mis-hitting. The ball never gets a chance to go where he aimed it. But even when hit squarely, the high-scoring shooter's ball goes horribly off line for no other reason than that's really where it was aimed.

The ability to drop your shot into a ten-yard circle from a couple hundred yards away involves a variety of skills which we'll go into later, but the procedure required to at least send the ball in the direction of the circle can be dealt with

Most duffers go about the lining-up procedure the wrong way round.

They march up to their ball. They set down their clubs to one side of it, select the weapon they're going to use, then approach the ball *sideways*. Then they go through all the preliminaries of getting ready to hit their shot.

And then they look at the target.

Brother, that is like standing in an elevator and trying to point your finger at Albuquerque.

The correct lining-up procedure starts when you are ten feet away from the ball, *behind it*. You position yourself so that your eye and the ball and the target are all on the same line. Then you march up to the ball as before—but your eye remains steadfastly fixed on the target. Forget about the ball completely. You can see enough of it out of the corner of your eye so that nobody is going to swipe it from you. Your thoughts now are on the target, and you should be concentrating on it with the same intensity with which, in a few seconds, you will be concentrating on the ball.

In other words, the shot-making process does not begin when you address the ball, but when you line up behind it.

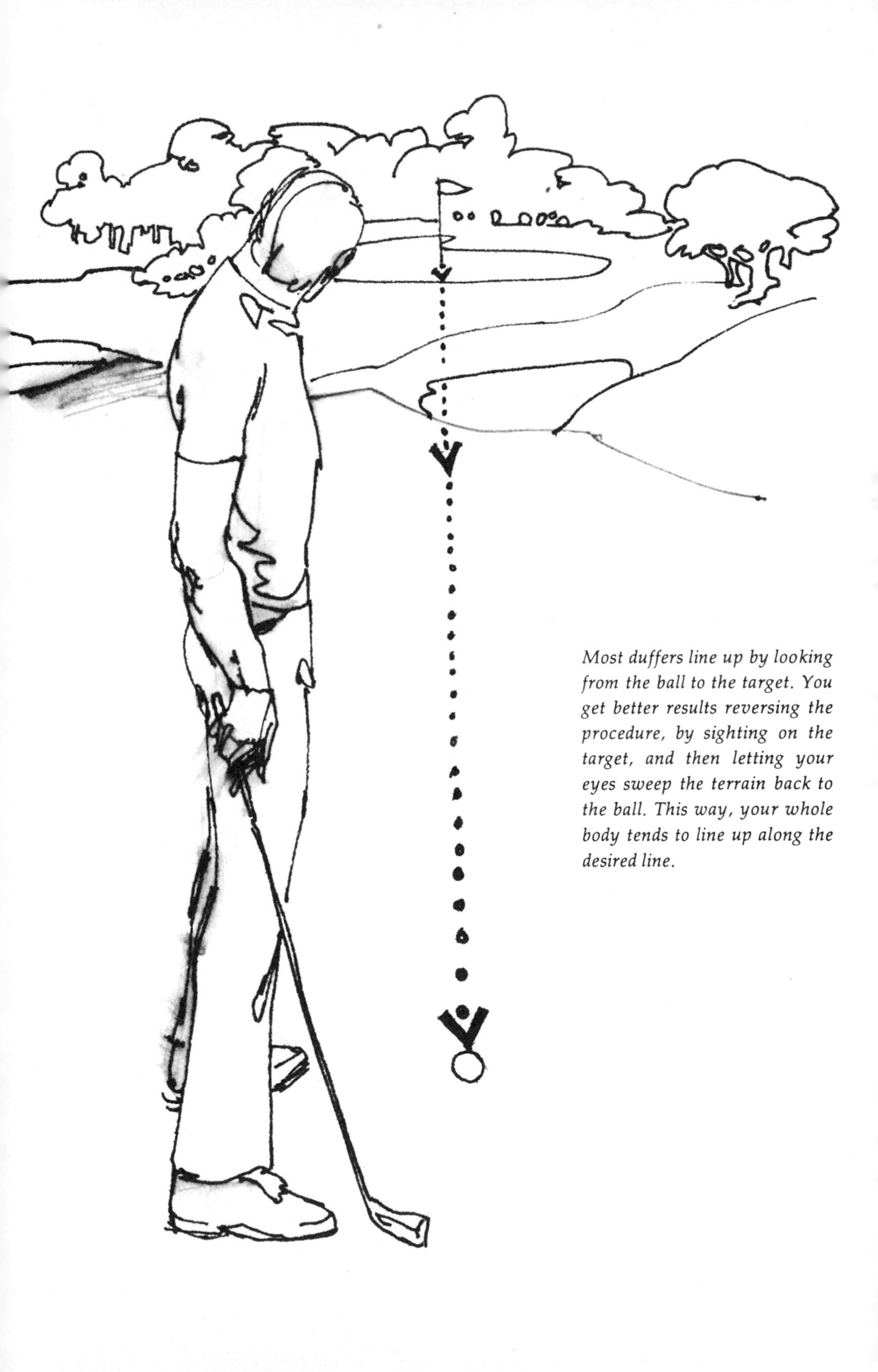

Most duffers line up by looking from the ball to the target. You get better results reversing the procedure, by sighting on the target, and then letting your eyes sweep the terrain back to the ball. This way, your whole body tends to line up along the desired line.

When you reach the position of address, with your eye still on the target, position your feet on that line which your senses tell you is absolutely parallel to the target. Don't ask me to explain the process which is taking place, because I can't. Neither do I know how I am able to shut my eyes and touch the tip of my nose. I just know I can do it through the help of some computer in my body—and it's the same computer which sends a message from my eyes on the target to my feet at the golf ball.

When your senses tell you that you are properly lined up, swing your eyes back from the target in a steady sweep which takes in all the geography between the two points. Probably you will still have to adjust a little to get the ball positioned correctly just back of your left heel, but the line of your stance in relation to the target will be dead-on. (Also, by "scanning" the topography from target to ball, you often can pick up a little extra information as to how the ball will bounce or roll in the last few yards to its stopping point.)

If you shuffle around a little and have to recheck your sighting, do not just look up from the ball and search out the target and let it go at that. Do the whole sweep over again. (It's the same in putting, incidentally; you check the line the ball must take to cover the last couple of feet into the cup, and work back from there, rather than starting out from the ball and working forward to the cup.)

The idea of letting your eyes sweep the line from target back to ball is that, by starting out from the distant object and coming back, the mental image of the flight path remains fixed in your mind, and so does the stopping area. This is a fairly new concept, and it's called "developing target image." Your mind can be trained to literally hold a picture of the target in your head while you are actually looking at the ball.

If you try it the other way around, from ball to target, you have to lift your eyes off the ball, losing that reference point, then hop around with your eyes until you find the target—

and the maneuver doesn't really accomplish anything.

I am spending a lot of time on this subject of direction, admittedly, but probably no more than the average duffer spends trying to develop his distance. Yet it is direction that gets the beginner into more trouble than will ever result from short-hitting. Having to chip on when you're short is a hell of a lot better than having to hack out from the jungle when you're off line.

The name of the game hasn't changed: it's still Keeping the Ball in Play.

Most duffers tend to lay the blame on the wrong doorstep when they send their shot off line. How many times have you played with a fellow who sends his shot 50 or 60 yards off line and then complains, "Oh, damn, look at that—I hooked it!" Yet he didn't hook it (or slice it) at all. The ball's flight was perfectly straight; it simply wasn't aimed right.

Again, if you are telling yourself that you have seen plenty of experts forego all this sighting business I have been stressing, you have simply been looking at some very lucky experts. And experts occasionally have to pay stiff penalties for mental lapses. A few weeks ago I played with a friend who is a beautiful nine-handicap golfer. And he was having a hell of a game. Without making one incredible shot, without making one fantastic putt—in other words, just playing good, steady, heads-up golf—he reached the eighteenth tee in 72 strokes. A par 4 would give him a very satisfying 76—which looked to be a cinch on a hole only 350 yards long, with a wide, forgiving fairway.

He belted his tee shot straight as an arrow, a good 240 to 250 yards. The way this guy could handle a wedge—and with the game certainly owing him a break with his putter—he had a real chance for a bird now.

I guess he was thinking that, too. And that little mental lapse—savoring his final score and not bearing down on the next shot—was all the fates needed. He didn't bother to line up his wedge, just took a few practice strokes until he felt he had just the right weight for the distance, then he stepped up to the ball and let fly.

Well, he was right about the weight, anyway. Pin high—right in the trap. No slice, no hook, the ball went right where his stance had aimed it. By the time he got out and down, his possible 75 had become a 78.

And I hear you saying, "If I could shoot 78, I wouldn't complain."

But that's the point, chaps. This very good golfer had had only one lapse in the round, and it had cost him at least two strokes. How many lapses do you suffer in a round? If they happen on the average of once a hole—well, you can see for yourself why that score can get up into the triple numbers. (Remember, the other name of the game is: It's Not Just Making Good Strokes, It's Eliminating Bad Ones.)

Golf requires fierce concentration, which is what the elimination of bad strokes is all about. And the concentration becomes all the tougher for the beginner, because he is faced with that awesome list of checkpoints he has to run through before he finally gets around to taking a whack at the ball.

But the list isn't quite so awesome if you approach the shot with only one question in mind:

How do I have to play this stroke to make absolutely sure the ball will be kept in play?

The answers we have discussed so far should then flood into your mind: your grip, your stance, your realistic assessment of the situation, and so on. These answers must be resolved before you move one millimeter into your actual swing.

SUMMARY

1. The ball is always hit off the left heel.
2. The weight is on the left foot more than the right.

3. Don't get onto your toes, always keep your weight on your heels.
4. Keeping the back straight, sag at the knees slightly as if "sitting down to the ball." This sets you up for the proper knee action, reduces the tendency to tip forward onto the toes, and gives your body a little slack to protect against being pulled off balance in the backswing.
5. Get used to the idea that you are going to place your feet no wider than shoulder width apart. In dufferdom, the big spread does not produce power.
6. Address the ball by taking a position along a line drawn from the target to the ball, not the other way around. Start off the lining-up procedure by approaching the ball from behind, along this imaginary line, rather than from the side.

You Can't Get Away With Murder

When the Counter Intelligence Corps of the United States Army back in Fort Holabird, Maryland, was teaching me how to pick locks, the basic tool of my handy-dandy burglary kit was a piece of spring steel known as a tension bar. The tip of it was bent at an angle of 90 degrees. When this tip was slipped securely into the keyway of a lock, you applied a gentle tension against the other end of the bar with the tip of your finger. The picking device would then flick the tumblers of the lock into line, and the tension created by the little piece of spring steel would turn the keyway and allow the lock to open.

Groovy. But what does this have to do with golf?

Well, it's one of the illustrations I am going to use which I hope will make clear to you what the golf swing is all about. I say "one of the illustrations" because it is my own experience that I can't always visualize something when given a single example, no matter how lucid that example may be. It may make perfect sense to one student, and be just a jumble of words to another, like trying to describe a spiral staircase without using your hands. Hopefully, out of a handful of illustrations, we will hit on at least one which will turn on the light for you.

So . . . when you approach the golf swing, think of yourself and your club as a giant-sized tension bar. The backswing is the application of tension, or torsion, or coiling up, and the downswing is the release.

At address, there is zero tension. But it starts to build up the instant you begin to move the clubhead back away from the ball. Reason: your feet remain fixed while your body twists. If you merely lift the clubhead, you are using a little strength to do it, but almost no torque. But by shoving the clubhead back along the grass, your body is taking on some of the characteristics of a spring. The further back you go, the tighter the spring is coiled, until you reach the top of the backswing and you can't coil any further. Also, there's no way you can hold that position for much more than a split second, because there's too much pent-up power to allow you to remain still.

So the downswing is a power-releasing motion, a smooth and natural build-up of momentum which starts with the pent-up energy of the coiling action and is then fed by the applied power of all the muscles of your body. The momentum reaches its maximum at the point of impact with the ball, and then expends itself smoothly and naturally in the follow-through.

Now please note:

Nowhere have I said that you take aim at the ball, rear back, and give it a wallop.

The downswing I have described is not a lunge at the ball, not a thing of brute force, but the natural release of energy. The perfect golf swing does not produce massive irresistibility like a charging tank, but lightning, constantly accelerating speed. It is a whipping action, caused by about one second of building up power through torsion, and a split second of releasing it. In terms of the amount of huff and puff expended, you seem hardly to have hit the ball at all.

And the fact is, *you* haven't hit it. You have brought the clubhead into the back of the ball as fast—not as hard—as you can, and the clubhead has done the hitting.

In this respect, golf differs from baseball. In golf you start off from zero tension, coil yourself up, and then unleash. The more smoothly you can control the process, the faster you can make the clubhead move at the moment it strikes the ball. In baseball you start with the bat at the shoulder, at the ready and with your rear foot already well braced. The explosiveness with which you lunge is produced to a large extent by sheer strength. Sure, there's plenty of wrist snap in a baseball swing, too, but the prerequisite is strength. Chi-Chi Rodriguez, at 125 pounds, doesn't have the strength to make it as a real slugger in baseball—but the way he can zing that clubhead into the golf ball has made him one of the top dozen or so long hitters in the game.

I only raise this point because I have seen so many beginners try to apply baseball power to golf, and it just doesn't work. They stand up to the ball with their feet wide apart, cock the club over their head, then bring it down into the ball with a hell of a smash. And they wonder—since the effort made them blow like a whale—why the ball didn't have any swift on it. Their trouble was that they attempted to make some of the elements of a baseball swing work for them, and they unconsciously started to hit the ball from the top of the swing. What happens when you do this is that the clubhead comes down into the impact area much too soon, way ahead of the rest of the body, and there just isn't any snap to its meeting with the ball.

It doesn't matter how big and strong a man is, he can't hit the ball through sheer power as far as a 97-pound weakling can send it through sheer clubhead speed.

This is tough to believe unless you can get some idea of the feel of golf power in your own body. So try this experiment.

Put down the *Guide* and stand up. For this exercise, you don't need a club. All you do is keep your body erect, with your feet shoulder-width apart and your arms at your sides. Now, really dig in with your toes, rolling inward slightly on the balls of your feet. This brings a slight amount of tension to the legs, not enough to create uncomfortable rigidity (because you keep your knees a little flexed) but at least enough to give you the clear sensation that your legs are there. (Remember, all of the body is involved in a good golf swing; if you can't feel any tension at all below the hips, it's very probably because you have fallen into the habit of using only your shoulders and arms to hit the ball.)

Now, turn your body into the backswing, with your arms still at your sides, relaxed, but applying as much torque as you can to your calf and thigh muscles. In other words, make an isometric exercise out of it, forcing your hips to turn into the backswing while forcing your feet to remain firmly clamped to the ground. Be very careful not to sway over to the right; just turn your hips.

Now let go.

If you've done it right, you torso will actually snap back to front and center. Keep on practicing until you can feel this snap.

If, after a few attempts, you still can't get any "bounce-back," probably your trouble is that you are not turning just your hips, you are turning your shoulders a bit as well. There's very little torsion built up this way, because you are distributing the tension over more of your body, and this dissipates the bounce-back.

But if you keep your shoulders square with your hips, turning no more than the hips allow, and keep digging in with your feet and calves, you should be able to suddenly relax the effort and feel your body snapping back to front and center.

This is a great exercise for getting the hang of how the hips and legs should function throughout the golf shot. Holding a club with the hands shoulder width apart, execute a full backswing of 90° using a twist of the knees and hips alone, keeping the shoulders completely square and without moving the arms. Now, swing all the way from this position, which is basically the top of the backswing, a full 180° to the left. Use only hips and legs, don't move arms or shoulders. Keep up the exercise in a steady back and forth motion until you can feel the power generated in a golf swing by hips and legs alone.

And this, of course, is where you're going to hit the ball, front and center, with your body helping you gain extra clubhead speed by its natural "bounce-back."

It may be that you still can't feel any particular sensation of snapping back, and I don't want to move onto new territory until you do. Unless you have a very clear understanding of the tremendous importance that hip action plays in the golf swing, you are not going to hit the ball with real authority.

Try this experiment. Hold a club in front of you, parallel with the ground, with your hands about 18 inches apart. Your arms should be extended straight out from your shoulders. Now, by hip action alone, without your arms and shoulders assisting, turn 90 degrees to the right. In other words, turn fully into the backswing. Now, turn a full 180 degrees to the left.

Keep up the exercise (Full Right, Full Left, Full Right, Full Left) until you are certain that your hips and only your hips are doing the turning. If it feels different from your first attempt at the isometric bounce-back exercise, you can bet that you have been hitting the ball mostly with the arms and shoulders, without making use of the full body snap of which you're capable. To work to best advantage, the snap must start with the knees and hips, with the arms and shoulders definitely trailing behind. The hands trail them, and the clubhead comes along last.

It's the old "crack-the-whip" principle from the kids' skating rinks. A dozen of them hold hands and get the line moving forward, all abreast, then the anchor man turns off at a tangent and the line of kids are snapped around in a circle until the twelfth kid is practically airborne. That twelfth kid is your clubhead. The anchor man is your feet and the number 2 and 3 men are your knees and hips.

THE CRACK-THE-WHIP PRINCIPLE. If you ever tried this as a child, you know that the faster the anchor man (at the bottom of the illustration) can start going back the other way, the faster the poor kid at the top end will find himself airborne. Think of the first half-dozen skaters as your lower body, driving into the shot, and you can visualize that if the kid at the end of the whip were a clubhead, it would have some swift on it when it meets the ball!

Here is another exercise which should be helpful:

Take the position we were using in Chapter Four to get the idea of the grip; that is standing at the position of address, with the arms pointed down at an imaginary ball and your palms pressed together. You should be bending slightly forward from the waist, with your knees flexed a little and your weight resting on your heels.

Now: keeping your feet flat on the ground, apply the same torsion to your lower body as before in the isometric exercise, and turn into the backswing.

Don't put too much muscle into that part of the movement which involves the arms and shoulders. Let the hips and knees do most of the work of turning. If you bring your arms and shoulders into it, there's the danger that you'll forget about your hips and merely copy the kind of swing known as "hitting from the top," in which the arms and shoulders take over much too soon to build up any real power.

Remember, too, since this simulates an actual golf swing, that your left elbow is straight, inside turned out, that your right elbow is slightly flexed and the inside cants slightly inward, and that the backs of both hands are pointing toward the target.

Now, when you get to the top of this abbreviated backswing, whip your hips from their Full Right position into the Full Left position. In other words, from backswing, through impact, into follow-through.

Do not try to do anything with your arms and shoulders.

If you did it right, you won't need to. The arms and shoulders will be whipped into the imaginary shot by the force of the hip-turn alone.

When I practice this little exercise, genteelly known as "getting your ass into it," I find my hands and arms fly straight out in a classic follow-through. If I don't keep a firm grip with my right hand, my left arm is pulled out of its grasp, whipping into the impact area and follow-through position by itself, through the sheer force of the hip-turn. I can't stop the arm. There's too much body momentum forcing it to whip into the imaginary shot.

Practice until you experience the same sensation, and you will learn a lot from this exercise. You will learn, for instance, that you really *are* doing what all the good golfers tell you you *should* be doing.

First, by keeping your eagle eye immovably fixed on the ball (real or imaginary), you will catch enough of a glimpse of your left shoulder to see that it really does tuck under your chin at the top of the backswing. (When you hit with bent elbows, the left shoulder only comes around as far as the left cheek, which isn't far enough.)

Second, your left knee will behave properly, too. From the flexed position at address, with your feet rolling inward slightly, the left knee will cock in, pointing toward the ball, because the action of the hips turning into the backswing will force it to do so. (If your knees are stiff, this doesn't happen.)

You will also discover that you actually get more steam on the downswing if you execute the backswing slowly rather than rushing it. All duffers rush their backswing, and I think the rush is triggered by the notion that the club must be whipped up into the air quickly if they are to maintain any sense of rhythm.

In fact, the opposite is true. The slower you can draw the clubhead back and around your shoulders, letting the whole process be guided by the building torsion of the knees, hips, shoulders, arms, and wrists, the more control you are able to maintain over your balance, and therefore the more perfectly you can time the reverse action when your knees and hips whip into the shot.

And after a while it may even occur to you that the arms function the most fluidly in this process when the left elbow is kept straight and the right elbow is tucked into the body all the way up into the top of the backswing. On the downswing, you should discover, you hardly have to think about the right elbow, because it seems to straighten itself out and into the shot at the correct moment, without any particular signal from your brain.

I am not saying all these things are going to happen the instant you try this exercise. If they did, a golf instruction

THE FORWARD PRESS. As *you can see, there's nothing to it. From Position A you simply press the wrists forward into Position B which gets your body moving very slightly, then as you straighten back to A, you just keep going into a smooth, tension-free backswing.*

book would need to run only about five pages. But what I do believe is that the whole secret of the golf swing is tied up in this one simple exercise.

It embodies the *essence* of the golf stroke, the fundamental truth that it is a swing and not a hit.

And this is the one big mental stumbling block in the path of the duffer. He finds it very hard to believe that, at some point in the exercise, he is not supposed to try to murder the ball. It is only when he has absorbed enough of the general instruction of golf, and applied it repeatedly to this little exercise, that he actually feels the power that a swing can generate—a swing that is triggered by his legs and hips, and not by his shoulders and arms.

There is tremendous grace in it, too, and you can feel it yourself if you turn the exercise into a pendulum maneuver, swinging not only from Full Right to Full Left, but back again from Full Left to Full Right. As you swing back to address from the follow-through, let the right hand catch the left again, and bring them both back into the backswing as a unit. This way, you get used to the automatic position of the body at all the positions, and—since your body is in motion from left to right—you get the feel of a really fluid take-away into the backswing.

The reason that the golf swing can accomplish so much in terms of driving the ball out of sight is that it reaches the peak of its efficiency at the point that the clubhead meets the ball—but it does not *end* at that point. You don't hit *at* the ball, you hit *through* it on the way to the completion of your swing.

Most beginners try to hit at *the ball instead of* through *it. As this illustration shows, the clubhead is still moving with tremendous power a good eight inches or so* after *the ball is hit—and along the same low line-drive trajectory. Unless you get used to trying to hit through the ball, nice and low, you may unconsciously start scooping at it, which results in those high, short-yardage bloopers.*

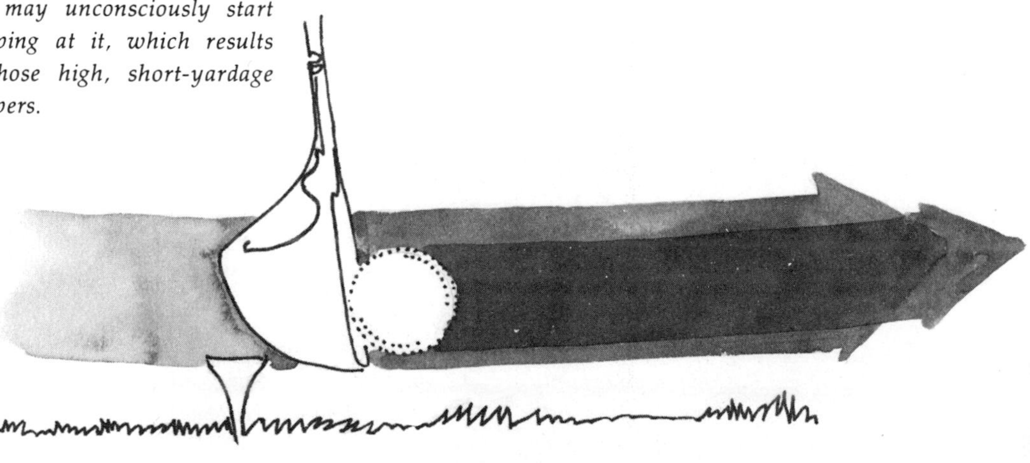

You will have taken a giant step toward improving your game when you come to understand, of your own experience, that hitting the ball is only an incident in the execution of the perfect swing.

I especially like this last exercise because it gets you thinking about all those random instructions you have read or been told about ever since you picked up your first club—phrases like "Keep your eye on the ball," "Turn the left knee into the ball," "Tuck your left shoulder under your chin," "Aim for a high finish in the follow-through," "Keep your left arm straight," and so on.

Most duffers think of these as style points. We speak of the great "style" displayed in the experts' swing. And frequently, if we get no further clarification, we are confused into thinking that style is like a coat of paint on a house—that it is an extra, which has nothing to do with the basic construction.

That is not true.

The classic cocking of the left knee, the full tuck of the shoulder, and so on are not mere points of style at all. They are what happen when you execute a good golf swing. And if they don't happen, you ain't doing it right. And let this be understood right now: It is not possible to noticeably improve your game by merely taking these components and slavishly tucking them onto your (ugh) regular swing. You can't go through the motions. The style points have to come naturally.

Now, let's get a club in our hands and see how it all works out in action.

Remember, we are trying to develop a stroke which is a symphony of smooth and fluid motion. In order to remove from your path the temptation to murder the ball, let us begin with one of the easiest of the clubs—the 5 iron—and leave the driver in the bag for the moment. What we are looking for here is the development of rhythm. Power comes later.

Pick up where you left off with the isometric exercise—pushing down with your feet, twisting back and away with knees, hips, arms, and shoulders. Now that you have a club in your hands, you will immediately notice that the feeling of torsion you felt before in your calves and thighs and hips—the torsion that produced the bounce-back—seems to have disappeared. This is because the tension is dispersed into the upper body, out through the arms and into the club itself (oh, yes, the club too is alive, as the bowed shaft demonstrates). The storehouse of power is still there, but you can't feel it until you apply torsion to the upper body and arms as well.

So let's do that. As you turn into the backswing with the lower body, start moving the clubhead back along the grass and up into a modest backswing, using only the left arm (or at least that's the way it feels) as the motive force. Make sure that you don't let the right hand get too much into the act. What we are striving for here is to get the sensation of the pendulum effect, and the right hand will just louse things up.

Take the backswing back only until your hands are hip high, feel the tug of the clubhead's weight as you arrest its backward swing, then reverse the arc of the pendulum by reversing your hips.

It should go like this: hip-turn right with left arm assisting, hip-turn left with everything relaxed. Keep it up until you achieve a nice, easy pendulum movement. Then gradually increase the amount of the turn of the hips, and the amount of the backswing of the left arm and shoulder, until you are taking about a three-quarters swing.

BUT—with every downswing, use only the hips and legs. Don't try to "hit" with the arms.

After a dozen or so of these pendulum swings (don't stop at the top of the follow-through, just swing backward in reverse flow), you should begin to experience a sensation known as "feeling the head of the club." This is the "tug of the clubhead's weight" I mentioned earlier, and when you feel it, you know you're doing it right, that you are letting your hips and your left side control the swing, and that you are not "hitting from the top" by bringing your arms and shoulders into dominance.

What is happening is that you are sending everything out in a smooth and unconstrained arc, then whipping it all back again with the snap of your hip-turn in the downswing. The clubhead is the last item in this crack-the-whip chain, and you can feel its weight out there. In an actual golf swing, delivered with some power, you get everything coming back into the downswing at such speed that the inert mass of the clubhead hangs there, fighting the reverse flow, and forces the shaft of the club to bend.

And this is what the big hit is all about—getting that bowed clubshaft back down into the impact area while it is still bowed. In the last dozen inches the bow straightens out, the clubhead is whipped forward at tremendous speed—and that ball is flattened!

If, instead, you try to hit from the top, the whole crack-the-whip action is foreshortened. Instead of the reverse flow starting from the bottom—from the knees and hips—it starts from the shoulders, and there simply isn't enough time or enough strength in the arms and shoulders to make up for the lost momentum of the hips and lower body. You're hitting it hard, agreed, but as the pros say, you've lost the swift, baby. The shoulders and arms come through the impact area ahead of the hips and lower body, forcing these real power sources to do no more than merely hitch a ride. The extra inertia slows down the impact speed, rather than increasing it.

I cannot stress too strongly the importance of the hips and knees. They *must* initiate the downswing, pulling the shoulders, arms, hands, club, and clubhead behind them. If they don't, the arms and shoulders can't wait around any longer in their coiled-up attitude at the top of the backswing, and they are forced to make the shot on their own.

As for the precise starting-point you use to initiate the downswing, that's up to you. Some golfers think of it in

The first four illustrations are slightly exaggerated to give you the feel of what is happening in that split-second from the top of the backswing to the moment when the wrists begin to uncock to lash the clubhead into the ball.

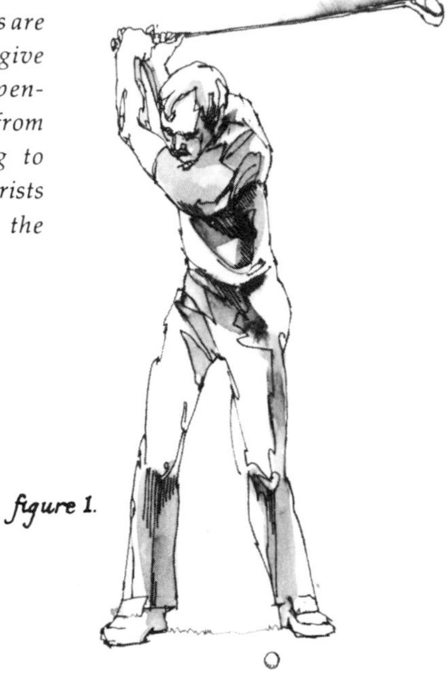

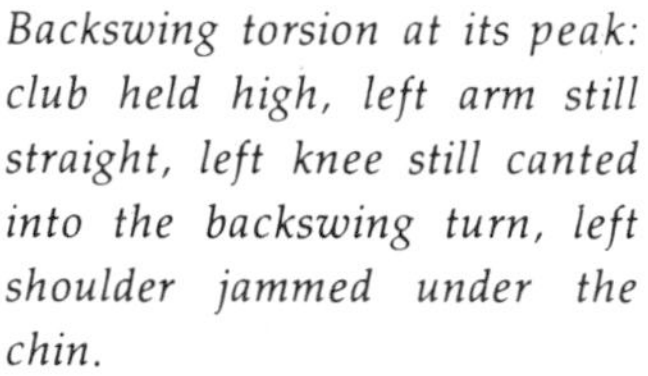

Backswing torsion at its peak: club held high, left arm still straight, left knee still canted into the backswing turn, left shoulder jammed under the chin.

Downswing release: right elbow tucked in tight, left arm dead straight in full control, left knee driving left hip out of the way of the shot, right foot, knee, thigh and hip driving into *the shot.*

terms of snapping the left knee into the ball, others think of driving the right knee into the left, others think of snapping the left hip out of the way, others think of driving the right hip into the shot.

I think of hitting the ball with my right buttock. It's the bump of the burlesque bump and grind. It may not get me into showbiz, but it sure gets me into the shot with full power.

Finally, I would like you to keep this in mind. Agreed, it is something of a drag to have to go through all this preliminary stuff before you get out there and really start hitting balls. But there is a real danger in trying to build up your tempo too quickly.

The trouble with leaping ahead without having absorbed the instruction thoroughly is that you start thrashing away at the ball without having any idea of what you're doing wrong.

)ownswing momentum: hips till twisting, left arm pulling he club down and into the ball, veight perfectly balanced, head teady, wrists fully cocked.

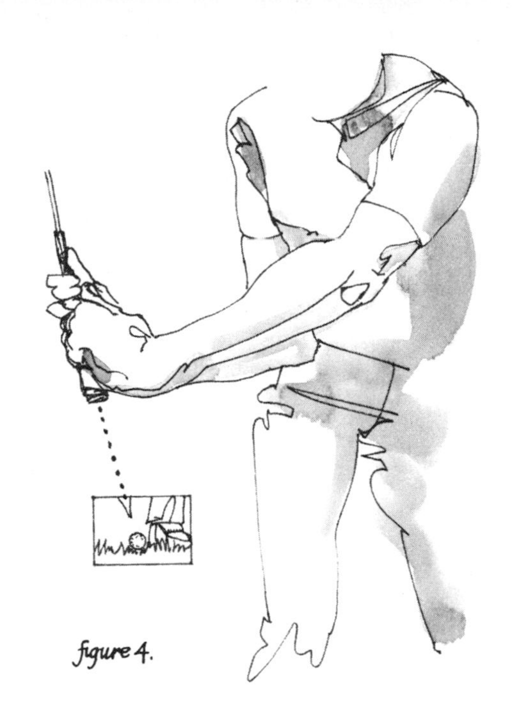

The body is more than half-turned into the shot, leaning into it, while the butt of the clubshaft is still aiming dead at the ball with the wrists still cocked.

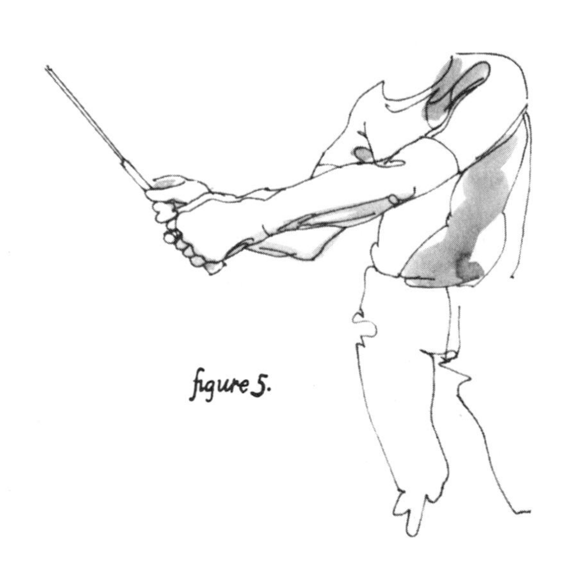

Compare this with Figure 4. On first glance, they look the same. But check the hips here: they have hardly begun to turn into the shot at all because the shoulders have come around too quickly. The left arm is straight, but the golfer has let his wrists uncock to the point where the butt of the shaft is already pointed well past the ball. In fact, regardless of where the clubhead is, he is "hitting" the ball now! When the moment of actual impact arrives, all of the steam of this shot will have evaporated. The golfer will think he has hit the ball hard, but it will take off with all the velocity of a dead duck.

The only way you can spot and correct mistakes—since you can't actually see yourself swing—is to know what the proper swing *feels* like.

My hope is that if you take it slow and easy at first, you will be able to practice power swings on the basis of sensations experienced or not experienced. If you know what the sensation is when the swing is executed leisurely, and you don't feel that same sensation under power, then you're short-circuiting it somewhere. That you can correct. But if you don't know—through at least 10 or 15 minutes of practice with these various pendulum exercises—what the right swing feels like, it is almost impossible to know what you're doing wrong under power because everything happens too quickly.

Unfortunately, it isn't enough to start off with the right grip and stance and so on, if you lose it all the instant you start to swing. You get so frustrated that you just stand up there and try to kill the ball, without swinging properly at all, and as this chapter title reminds us, there's just no point in doing that—because in golf you can't get away with murder.

SUMMARY

1. Concentrate on developing a proper swing and forget about trying to hit the ball.
2. Start the backswing by moving the knees and hips into the turn; start the downswing the same way. Do not start either process with the shoulders.
3. Practice your exercises until you can feel the clubhead weight at the top of the backswing, and all the way through the downswing. If you can't feel the weight of the clubhead, you have lost your crack-the-whip momentum.
4. With the feet firmly planted, develop a full body twist, which provides the initial momentum for the knees and hips to whip into the downswing.
5. Remember, start your take-away by shoving the clubhead back across the grass, and not by lifting it over your head.

Tell Yourself What Not to Do

Knowing what I know now, if I were to take up golf all over again, I would spend very little money on books and all the money I could with a real live professional teacher. The trouble with books is that you can't ask them a question.

I believe, too, that the beginning golfer can become very frustrated by any instruction which, no matter how lucid it may be, is limited to the positive: "Do this."

I think there's a lot to be said for the negative: "Don't do that."

What I base this on is the reaction of most beginners to the kind of instruction that tells them only the right way of doing things. The reaction is, "But that's the way I *am* doing it!"

All too often, the student is not doing it the right way, but how is he to know? He has nothing to compare with, no element he can reject.

This is why I think it will be valuable to spend some more time discussing what is wrong with hitting from the top. If you are able to identify it when it happens to you, and if you are then able to compare it with what should be happening in the proper golf stroke, it seems to me it should be a lot easier to get the bad habit out of your system.

First let's review the proper golfing stroke and how it is achieved.

The hands grip the club in such a way that the back of the left hand and the palm of the right point directly toward the target.

The left arm is straight, with the inside of the elbow pointing out from the body, and there is very little bend in the line from the left shoulder to the clubhead. The right arm is bent, relaxed, with the right elbow held comfortably close to the body. Both hands are turned down at the wrists, as if firing six-shooters into the ground in front of you.

Because the left arm is straight and the hand is turned down, and because it is kept that way throughout the swing, you cannot pick the clubhead off the grass. All you can do is shove it backward.

Because the left side controls the backswing in this sweeping or shoving motion, the clubhead is forced to take the long way round to the top of the swing. And because the left side will control most of the return trip, save the last 12 inches of the impact area, the clubhead will benefit from a very long arc in its downward path, thereby picking up more and more speed.

Because the downswing is initiated at the hips, with the clubhead being the last segment of the chain to get the message, the inertia caused by the clubhead's weight resisting the reversal of direction will cause the shaft to bend.

Because the golfer's wrists are the second last segment of the chain to experience the crack-the-whip effect, and because they experience this effect just as they enter the impact area, they will be forced to uncock with great power.

Because the wrists uncock at this precise moment, the bowed shaft will be forced to straighten out with a vicious snap, which will tremendously increase the speed of the clubhead as it encounters the back of the ball.

Because the speed of the clubhead is so great, and because there is still momentum in the body, the clubhead will shoot out toward the target until it reaches the limit of the golfer's extended arms, eventually bringing the whole body around into what is known as the high finish.

The golfer's navel will be aimed directly at the target, and the ball will go rocketing toward its goal as if fired directly from the belly button.

The ball will go straight because the golfer's feet were properly positioned to send it straight, and because the golfer's hands brought the face of the clubhead into the back of the ball in a perfectly square position.

Hurray! Now, let's see what happens when we do it wrong.

First, the hands grip the club in a position which makes it easier to lift the clubhead off the grass rather than sweep it backwards.

Because the arms are able to lift the clubhead up rather than move the clubhead around the body, they continue to do so by bending the elbows, taking the line of least resistance.

Because the bent arms no longer need the left hip to help

Here's where it's all gone wrong. The left elbow has become so fully bent to get the club over the head that the very action of straightening the left arm in the downswing will pull the clubhead into an outside-in arc. And that means, at best, a rather horrible slice.

shove the clubhead into its arc, the hips are left virtually stationary, still at the position of address.

Because the whole body has not been employed in the big, extended arc of a full backswing, the swing is more of a loop than an arc, more of a circle than an ellipse, and the clubhead is sent—not around the turned shoulders—but over and behind the head.

Because there is almost no turned body to turn back (it remained more or less at the position of address), the golfer has no other alternative than to start hitting the ball from the top of the swing, using only his arms and shoulders, producing force rather than momentum.

Because the clubhead was over and behind the golfer's head at the top of the swing, it returns along the same path, finally meeting the ball along a line known as "outside-in" —which means that the clubhead crossed the downswing, and then met the ball as it again crossed the intended line of flight on its way inside.

Because this outside-in downswing allowed the clubface to slide across the back of the ball at the moment of impact (rather than meeting the back of the ball squarely), the ball started off with a clockwise spin on it.

Because the clubface cannot be effectively kept square with this kind of swing, it was allowed to fall open, increasing the loft of the clubface and increasing the clockwise spin, and also adding bottom spin.

Because it is spinning up and to the right, the ball will go up and to the right.

Because we will probably never see it again, I hope you brought along plenty of spares.

I suppose this might be considered funny if it were not for the fact that I have not exaggerated anything. In fact, I have at least given this all-too-frequent chain of events the benefit of the doubt and assumed that the golfer hit the ball. Usually when a swing breaks down you can count on either a complete miss or lifting up a foot of turf before you even get to the ball.

This is precisely what happened: the swing broke down. It lost all of its smooth, pendulum sweep and disintegrated into a choppy, uncoordinated attack on the ball.

If this is happening even after you have tried to put the instructions in this *Guide* to work for you, I suggest you concentrate on three main points: the grip, the speed of the backswing, and the action of the knees and hips.

If your hand, wrist, and arm positions are correct at address, it should be easier to shove the clubhead back along the grass and turn the body with it, than it is to lift the clubhead over your head.

Incidentally, you hear a great deal about cocking the wrists and where to uncock them, and where not to uncock them. I'll let you in on something. If you start off with the right grip, and if you have a definite feeling of clubhead weight at the top of the downswing, your wrists perform the magic of cocking and uncocking all by themselves, without any conscious effort on your part.

As for the speed of the backswing, almost every duffer errs on the side of too fast. I don't know if it's possible to do it too slowly, but you can certainly do it too quickly.

I think the trouble stems from not knowing precisely how to start the shot off. It's difficult to instruct on this point because, with proficiency, the motion becomes such a fluid blend that it's hard to tell which precise muscle started the chain reaction.

This is probably why so many good golfers use "the forward press," because it tends to get everything working at once. The forward press is just a sophisticated form of the old "waggle," which was very popular a few years ago as a tension reliever. The waggle was a shifting of the weight from hip to hip, after the fashion of a hula dancer, and the thing you tried to do was to go into the wind up right at the end of the waggle, before your stationary pose got you all tensed up. The forward press is a big improvement on it. All it calls for is a slight lean to the left with the hips and the hands—pressing forward, in other words—and as you pull back to erect, instead of coming to a stop you just keep on going into the backswing. When you're trying to put everything all together, it's a bit difficult to get the hang of it, but I recommend giving the forward press some practice as early as possible because it definitely promotes knee and hip movement.

You can easily tell if you're too fast in the backswing. It promotes hysteria. Really. You whip the club back so fast that you lose all mental and physical sense of rhythm and timing. You find yourself up there at the top of the backswing without knowing exactly where you are or how you got there—or how to get down gracefully. Panic replaces coordination in an instant. Slow down the backswing, and the panic goes away. So will your tendency to slice, top, whiff, and blaspheme.

Think of it this way. When you become a competent golfer, you can maintain the correct arc of the club and the correct order of events even with a fairly brisk backswing. You can do it because, on the way to becoming competent, your mind and your body have learned how to do the right thing by reflex.

While you're still learning, all you can do by reflex is make mistakes. What you do right happens only because you've thought about it, been deliberate, even exaggerated. But don't let that worry you. Exaggeration goes away as soon as you begin to recognize the feel of doing it right. If you try whipping back the clubhead with blinding speed, everything happens so quickly that you can't feel anything at all.

It must be so slow and smooth and stately that when the top of the swing is reached, your mind isn't cluttered by any flashing lights of apprehension. All you are thinking about is the hip-turn which will start the downswing.

Remember that you are thinking about the hip-turn, not about "getting back down again." If you snap your knees and hips into the downswing with plenty of authority, all the other parts of the chain will get down by themselves. The hips pull them there.

If you find that you are lifting your left heel off the ground in the backswing, you are edging closer to getting yourself off balance, and you are probably swaying with the shot. The more you sway to the right, the tougher it is to get back over to the left where the ball is. When you start off with the weight toward the left side, as we discussed earlier, there is no reason for the left heel to lift.

Nor will you ever lose your balance if your weight is properly distributed and you avoid the disastrous habit of hitting from the shoulders. Some men can swing from the shoulders so violently they actually fall down.

An easy way to spot the shoulder swinger is in his practice strokes. As I have said, when you hip-turn full right in the backswing and full left in the follow-through, with your navel aimed squarely at the target at the finish, you have exhausted the whole momentum of the swing in a natural and balanced way. But if you don't hip-turn, the clubhead does not follow the ball to the target. It is trying to wrap itself in a tight coil around your head. To avoid being decapitated, the shoulder-swinging golfer does a funny little loop with the club at the end of the swing, to exhaust its momentum. At least, that's what he does in practice. In a real swing he is hitting so hard with his shoulders that he can't get the loop working for him and he has to keep corkscrewing his body to get out of the way of the clubhead. Eventually he is pulled right off his feet.

This is usually the problem of the heavyset man. He has plenty of strength, but he doesn't think he has much maneuverability in the hips and beam department, so he attempts to swing completely from the shoulder. His hips don't move an inch. And because he has the upper-body strength, he whips his arms into the shot so violently that he has to involuntarily duck his head in his follow-through, for fear his own arm is going to take it off.

The fact is, the heavyset man should be relying especially on his hips, rather than ignoring them. His torso gets in the way of a really full lateral arm movement, but he has no difficulty in getting his hips to turn to make up for his restricted arm movement. What he should try is a swing which takes a much flatter plane than normal, positioning himself a little further away from the ball than the man with the average build. Thus, he can both see the ball without difficulty, and swing at it smoothly as well. What every golfer should be trying to achieve, you see, is the most compact swing his body is suited to. The heavier fellow gets maximum compactness by swinging flatter and getting a little further away from the ball. But never does he reach for it on tippy-toe. Because of his weight, it is all the more important that he be settled firmly on his heels.

The tall, lanky golfer has the reverse problem. His tendency is to get everything stretched out in order to accommodate his height and arm length. The trouble is, he gets it too spaced out. He should work on a super-compact swing with as upright an arc as possible, because his arm length gives him all the extension he will need, and his necessity now is to keep "tight to the ball."

In both cases, a visit to a pro shop is a good idea, to find out if your clubs have the proper lie for your kind of swing.

The tall fellow needs a more upright lie than normal; the overweight man needs it less upright.

SUMMARY

1. When you're trying to correct a fault, work at it from both directions simultaneously. Tell yourself what you have to do—but also tell yourself what not to do.

2. This chapter contains two lists: why it went right, and why it went wrong. Learn both of them. After every shot you should be able to say, "Because I did such and such, so and so happened." It will strengthen your strong points and make you aware of your weaknesses in a constructive way.
3. Become practiced in the forward press. It makes for a much smoother take-away than trying it cold, from an absolutely stationary position.
4. Slow down your backswing. That ball isn't going anywhere until you hit it.
5. When you reach the top of the backswing, don't start to hit the ball. Turn your hips instead. It's the only way to get back down again smoothly.

Putting It All Together

Is golf only one of several recreational interests with you?

If so, you have probably never experienced a fairly common occurrence among avid golfers; they dream about the perfect swing.

They fall asleep, not by counting sheep or General Motors shares, but by touring their favorite course in an absolutely exquisite round.

Bobby Nichols admits that he dreams of the perfect swing, except that it isn't his (so *he* says; I'd sell state secrets to have Nichols' swing). The strokes he dreams of belong to Sam Snead and Ben Hogan.

George Knudsen dreams of a perfect stroke which nobody owns. He has said that his mind is filled with this vision of the most beautiful golf stroke in the world, delivered time after time with constant, unvarying perfection. I myself have seen a serious golf teacher staring rapturously at stop-frame photography of classic golf strokes with the kind of fascination the rest of mankind reserves for the *Playboy* gatefold.

But none of these gentlemen, or any other serious devotee, ever seems to spend much time rhapsodizing about how far the ball travels when it is dispatched by the dream hit.

You see, it isn't important how far it goes.

If it is given a perfect hit, it will go far enough. It will leap from the turf with a rich, full-bodied *click;* it will sail up into

The urge is over-powering, isn't it? And the results are disastrous usually, aren't they? So the gods of golf must be trying to tell us something—and they are. There is just no way you can murder the ball and maintain the necessary smoothness and control that makes for straight long hits. So get the larceny out of your heart.

the sky in a rising arc, as dead-on target as a guided missile (which of course it is); and when the sphere again meets the ground, it will either bite and stop dead, or roll smoothly forward, all as the man who hit it willed.

With such beautifully lyric thoughts as these should your mind be filled, as you loom above the golf ball at the top of the backswing.

But if, instead, your brain shrieks, *Kill!* and you lunge at the ball as if to murder it . . . well, then, sir, you are a fink.

And you will be paid back with a lousy shot. If murder is in your heart, no good will come of it.

The ball can be hit straight and far *only* when it is thought of in a secondary way, as an obstacle in the path of a beautiful swing. If it is the primary thought, with all else in the swing relegated to second place (and dimly second, at that) you may get off some sort of bloopy shot, but you are far more likely to cut an ugly smile in the face of your ball, or an ugly trench in the fairway turf.

Let us press on, then, to discuss the path of the beautiful swing.

As you will recall from an earlier chapter, Arnold Palmer has said that all he concerns himself with in his swing is the first 12 inches of the backstroke. If he can keep the clubhead low and smooth in his backward sweep, he knows that all else is well.

It is in the first 12 inches of the take-away that two of the basic elements of a good swing can be clearly observed.

The first and most obvious is that if the clubhead is still close to the grass, then you must be shoving it back, properly, rather than lifting it, improperly. The second element which can be observed is that, in the last three or four inches of that first foot of take-away, the clubhead is already beginning to pull inside the line of flight, making it not only possible but natural for it to come down into the ball again from inside-out.

(The reason that these observations can be made only in the first 12 inches, of course, is that your eye remains fixed on the ball, and the clubhead begins to fade out of focus when it's about a foot away from the ball.)

Is Arnold Palmer correct, then? Can you be confident of a good hit if you concentrate on getting that first 12 inches right?

Yes and no. Yes, definitely, if the other components of the swing are correct. But you're still not out of the woods—even if you execute what looks like a perfect swing—if you have not paid proper attention to your grip.

You see, even if your position at the top of the backswing looks absolutely classic, if the way you are holding the club is faulty then the clubface will not be in the correct attitude—even though everything else seems to be—when it meets the ball.

Try it for yourself.

Take your 5 iron and execute a slow-motion backswing, as absolutely perfectly as you can:

- Start with a grip that's square to the target.
- Slowly sweep the clubhead into the backswing.
- Let your turning body and straight left arm carry it around your shoulders.
- Keep your right elbow close to your right ribs.
- Turn into the downswing by starting with your knees and hips.
- Let your straight left arm pull the club toward the impact area.
- Finally, straighten your right elbow and let your uncocking wrists bring the face of the club to the exact point where it should encounter the ball.

Then stop.

If you have done everything properly, your body and arms and hands will be way out in front of the ball, turned fully into the shot—but the clubface will be exactly as it was at address, absolutely square.

(Incidentally, you may have to do this a few times before you can get the clubface to come back square. This is because it's tricky to be keeping everything smooth when you're doing it in slow motion.)

Now, purposely take a new grip on the club and, as much as you can, exaggerate a poor grip. Let your hands come up on top of the shaft so that the back of the left hand and the back of the right are both pointing almost as much toward the sky as they are toward the target.

Even with this poor grip, adjust the clubface until it is

lined up perfectly to hit the ball dead square.

Now repeat the slow-motion swing, again trying to do everything with absolute perfection. Come to a stop at the point of impact and look at your clubhead.

It is wide open.

(At least it is if you didn't anticipate what was going to happen and sneak in a little hand adjustment during the swing—which is almost impossible to do during the split second of a real swing.)

What you're trying for in the development of a good golf swing is a miniature version of what you're trying for in a good golf game—the elimination of those elements which are going to get you into trouble. Sure, by a series of compromises and contortions you can ignore everything I've been saying and still get the odd good shot away. There's a guy who can even smack the ball 200 yards down a fairway while seated in a kitchen chair. Anything, I suppose, is possible. But if it's probability you're looking for, then all of the components of the swing which I've been talking about are your best insurance. They are a combination of interlocking, mutually complementary techniques which are the best that man has been able to devise over the course of several centuries of trying to make little white balls go straight and far when hit with crooked sticks.

Everything is a crucial element—the grip, the stance, the swing, the weight distribution, the head movement, etc., etc., etc. Is it any wonder, then, with all these things to think about, that the really good golfer is reluctant to try to murder the ball? Just to hit it with reasonable accuracy and authority is problem enough, without trying also to extend yourself beyond the limits of smoothness and tempo and timing.

And this brings us almost to the end of what you have to know about Putting It All Together.

Gary Player was once quoted as saying, in regard to a particular shot, that he had hit it with everything he had. Now, as most golf fans know, Player is a real physical culture buff; he's in fantastic condition and as strong as an ox. But when he talks about hitting it with everything he has, he doesn't mean he's trying to kill the ball.

He means that he is forcing the safety factor of *his ability to swing smoothly* to its ten-tenths limit.

In this terminology, most pros summon up only eight- or nine-tenths of their ability to swing smoothly, even when they are going for a very distant target. As the great English racing driver Stirling Moss used to say about Grand Prix driving, you need nine-tenths to be superb, ten-tenths to be fantastic, eleven-tenths to be dead.

Most duffers try for eleven-tenths with almost all their distance shots—and they pay for it horribly. Yet, ironically, most duffers can get eminently respectable "average golfer" distances employing only six- or seven-tenths of their ability to swing smoothly.

Let us examine this carefully.

There are three basic ingredients in the long shot. As I have mentioned several times, the primary element is clubhead speed. Hit the ball as hard as you like, but if your hard hit doesn't develop top speed at the clubhead, all you're doing is wearing yourself out. The impact feels and sounds leaden, and the ball's flight in the air looks somehow strained, as if the ball is fighting to keep aloft.

Coupled with clubhead speed are two other basic necessities. The clubhead must travel in the proper arc to meet the ball as squarely as possible—to send it straight—and the clubface must meet the ball at the angle of loft for which the club was designed. Otherwise, it may go straight and have plenty of zip, but it goes so high in the air that it doesn't go as far as it should along the ground.

The problem, then, is: How do I get the clubhead moving quickly at impact, while bringing it to the point of impact along the right trajectory and keeping the face of the club at the correct angle of attack?

The solution: by making sure I have everything perfectly positioned at address, and then by swinging so smoothly that nothing gets out of position during the second or so between address and impact.

It ain't easy. The clubhead travels more than 20 feet in the average swing, and that's plenty of distance in which to get into trouble. The more you add to that distance by going all out, by overswinging, in fact, the more you increase the possibility of error. Most duffers are edging into the danger area at even 80 or 90 percent of their potential, but they can handle about 60 percent and hit the ball beautifully.

Your own experience proves it. Think of some beautiful shot you pulled off when, for one reason or another, you declined to hit the ball with your usual, ahem, mighty blast. Damned if the thing didn't take off like a bird and fly 30 or 40 yards more than you'd hoped for. And when it happened, chances are you turned to your partner and said something like, "Wow, look at that—and I just barely hit it!"

RIGHT!

That's the point! You don't need to hit it hard to make it go far!

I will admit that this is extremely hard to believe while you're still getting poor results from hitting the beast as hard as you can. Your natural response is: How can it possibly go further when it's hit softer? The answer is: It doesn't go further because it was hit softer, but because it can usually be hit smoother when it's hit softer—and smoothness generates clubhead speed. When you're smooth you're in control, and it's the control—or tempo or timing or whatever word you want to give it—which allows you to snap your straightening right forearm and your wrists into the shot just as they enter the impact area.

Assuming, then, that you understand the physics of clubhead speed, let's go on to the path of the clubhead and the angle of its face at its meeting with the ball.

We have already covered the inside-out flight path in some detail. It's achieved by shoving the clubhead back along the grass in the first foot of the take-away, which in turn is achieved by turning into the backswing with a straight left arm around the pivot of a bent right arm. When the clubhead comes down and around your body the same way, the face of the club covers the last six or eight inches of the downswing, immediately before it meets the ball, on exactly the same line as the intended line of flight of the ball. Only after the hit does the clubhead cross over the intended line of flight, as momentum sweeps it up into the follow-through.

If, as we have explained, the clubhead meets the ball while moving from outside the line of flight to inside it, it cuts across the back of the ball and puts a clockwise spin on it, producing a slice.

Tied directly into the need to come up on the ball from the right direction is the need to keep the clubface square. If the clubface falls open, the degree of loft is tremendously increased, and even though the club you're using may be a 3 iron, you're giving it 9-iron loft. Moreover, the heel of the club comes into the ball ahead of the toe, and the ball is given a tremendous additional clockwise spin and thrust to the right. So that's were it goes.

These maladies are the most common afflicting the duffer. He's usually a horrible slicer. And these are some of the popular remedies he comes up with to correct (he prays) the problem.

1. Aiming the shot at a 45 degree angle to the left, in the hope that there will be enough left-side compensation to keep the ball somewhere on the fairway when it comes slicing back to the right. Some golfers get fairly adept at this. They go up and down the fairways shooting semicircles.
2. Toeing in the clubhead. The face of the club at address is inclined 45 degrees or so to the left, in the hope that when it comes down from the top of the outside-in backswing it will meet the ball more or less flush. This is called Two Wrongs Trying to Make a Right. Unfortunately, if you occasionally swing properly, the clubface meets the ball

at that weird toed-in angle—and off it goes, dead left.

Depressing, isn't it? And the situation is not going to change until you can get it thoroughly fixed in your mind that the clubface must be kept square throughout the swing.

"But damn it all," you protest, "I *am* keeping it square!"

Throughout the swing?

Ay, there's the rub. How does the golfer know the face is remaining square once he starts into the backswing and can no longer keep his eye on it?

Only by swinging smoothly, so he maintains the feeling in his hands and wrists.

Try this. Take a couple of slow swings with the idea of accomplishing nothing else but keeping the clubface square. Now try one and stop at the top of the backswing. While you hold the club up there, have a friend grasp the clubhead (it's easier with an iron than a wood) and tip the toe of the clubhead up toward the sky, while you hold your grip firmly enough that your shaft doesn't turn in your hands.

Hey, hey! Feel something? Is your friend's twisting of the toe of the club forcing your left hand and wrist to come up on top of the shaft? It is? Well, guess who hasn't been keeping the clubface square throughout the swing.

The first few times you try this, there is usually the sensation of awkwardness, of being cramped in the backswing. That's mostly because you've probably been overswinging. The club is supposed to go back only as far as the turning body, the straight left arm, and the unbroken left wrist will allow.

If it goes back any further, you're unconsciously cheating, breaking down the swing in order to get the club back further. One or all of the following is happening:

The left wrist is breaking.

The left elbow is bending.

The right elbow is flying away from the body instead of remaining close to the right ribs.

Don't be disturbed if the correct positions and movements feel unnatural at first. To repeat, there is nothing particularly natural about a golf swing. It is an aquired skill. Only when the golfer has mastered it does it feel completely comfortable—and then, happily, the good swing feels completely natural and the poor swing feels awkward.

Consider, since we've mentioned it, the right elbow. If you stick it out, you can't bring the club back and around the body. Try it yourself. Stop halfway through the backswing and lift your elbow away from your body. See how it sends the clubhead over your head, on an outside-in path? Tuck it back, and the swing flattens again.

Now consider the breaking wrists. Go to the top of the backswing with your driver, with the wrists straight and unbroken. Now break your left wrist and you can get the clubhead to dip well below the horizontal. But you're not taking a bigger swing that way, all you're doing is allowing the pent-up energy of torsion (see Chapter Six) to dissipate itself in an overswing.

Finally, consider the bent left elbow. If you have fallen into the habit of bending it to get the backswing started (lifting the clubhead, rather than shoving it backward), what do you do to get the downswing started? You straighten the left elbow, *naturellement*. And what does that do? My, my, it seems to force the whole crack-the-whip action to reach its peak when your clubhead is still approximately a yard from the ball. Or, as they say, you have hit from the top. Which is a no-no.

The vital factor in a really powerful golf swing is an event which is known as the late hit.

Simply, it means that the moment when the clubhead strikes the ball is as late as you can possibly make it.

After your knees and hips have driven through the shot.

After your shoulders and arms.

After your wrists and hands.

After every bone and muscle in your body has functioned in its proper sequence to build up clubhead speed, then, and only then, should impact occur.

One of the most effective ways to develop a late hit is to try to aim the butt of the shaft at the ball as long as you can in the downswing. If your straight left arm is ramming the butt down at the ball, obviously the clubhead is being held back. Furthermore, the ramming-down-with-the-butt tends to force you to keep your wrists cocked to the very last instant.

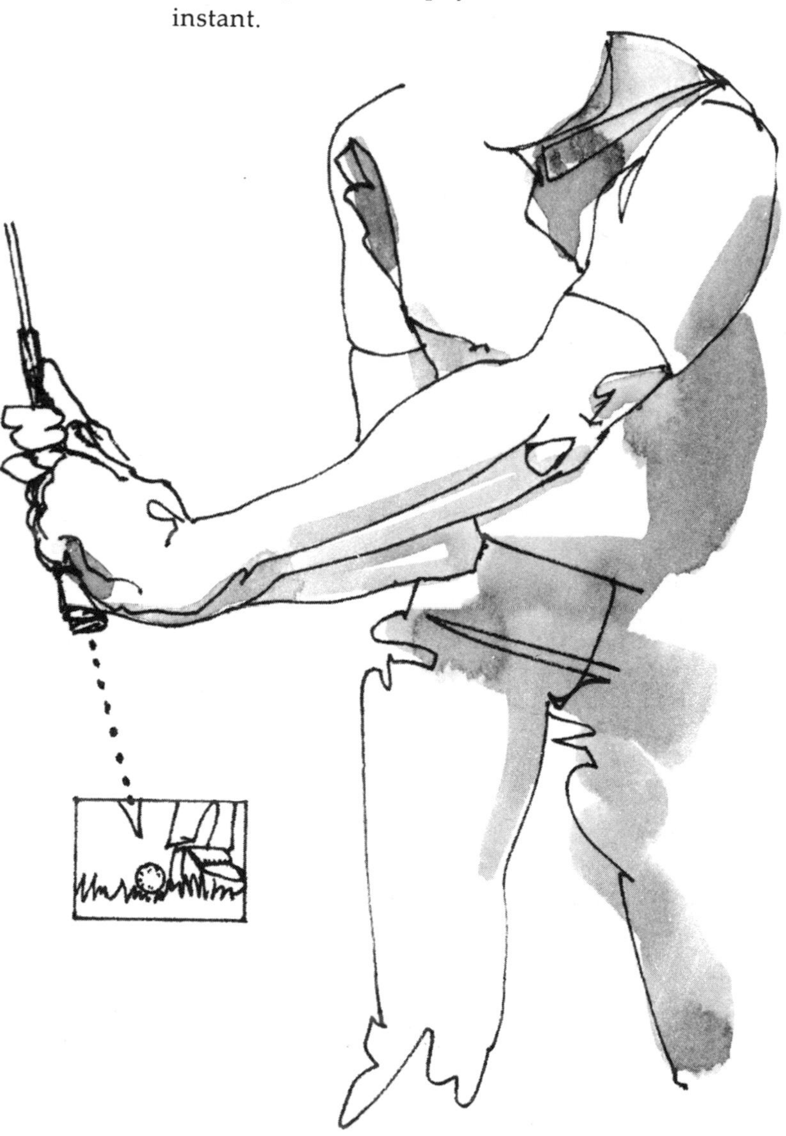

And the combination of getting your body into the shot first, while ramming down with the butt, is a perfect solution to remedy any tendency you may have to try to scoop up the ball. The attempt to scoop at the ball can work only if the body is late and the clubhead comes through first. If the clubhead is forced to come through last, it smashes down and through the ball, exactly as it should, and only the built-in loft of the clubface does the lifting. Which means that all of the clubhead speed is used in sending the ball over the ground, and not wasted in sending it up into the air.

Both lunging and scooping, though, are as much problems of the mind as they are faults of the swing. They come from thinking about hitting at the ball, rather than thinking about executing a perfect swing. Do not, as I have said before, try to make the point of contact with the ball a moment of any special meaning. Above all, don't fall into the habit of letting your shot end at the point of contact. Don't hit at the ball at all. Hit through it.

This applies to every stroke in the repertoire. You hit through the ball just as much in the putting stroke or the delicate little chip or the recover from a bunker as you do off the tee with your driver.

In every shot, you must let momentum take its natural course. You must say to yourself: I am executing a golf swing, and the ball is only an incident in the course of that swing.

If you are thinking more about the hit than the swing, you are heading for trouble, especially in the short game. Nothing drives you into a rage of frustration faster than using up three or four strokes to cover a distance of ten yards—because all you're thinking about is hitting the ball, not completing the swing, and all you keep doing is stubbing your club into the ground while the ball skitters forward no more than a couple of yards. That problem we'll deal with in Chapter Ten.

Before we end this chapter on putting it all together, there is one point of your physical equipment that we have not yet discussed.

Your head.

Mirror, mirror, on the wall, in my shorts I'm ten feet tall! . . . So how come I'm so lousy on the course? (Tension mostly. When we practice at home, we concentrate on the swing, and there it is, a thing of beauty. When we get on the course, we get that old kill-the-ball feeling. Remember: The swing's the thing, forget the ball—and that's what makes you ten feet tall!)

We have talked a good deal about using your brains, but not much about what you are supposed to do physically with your head. And the answer is: as little as possible.

I hesitate to tell you that you shouldn't move it, because some beginners accept this instruction literally to the point of holding their head and neck so stiffly that they create muscular tension throughout their whole body, which makes it almost impossible for anybody to swing smoothly.

So let's try it this way: You can move your head as much as you want, as long as you keep your eye on the ball, and as long as the movement of your head does not force any other part of your body to move with it.

Which, as you can appreciate, does not give you very much freedom of head movement.

But, you may ask, just exactly why should I not move my head?

There are two general reasons. First, if you move your head back along the path of the backswing, it means that you are swaying over to the right and not keeping your weight directly over the ball. I mentioned earlier that the swing pivots around the bent right elbow, and that's true; but the *body* also pivots—around a centerline which is the middle of the triangle created by your head and your feet. What you must practice to perfection is looking down at the ball with fierce visual concentration while allowing your body to pivot freely beneath the permanently fixed point, which is your head. As the downswing moves into the follow-through, your right shoulder comes *under* your chin and carries it around to face the target. And that's the only time you allow your head to move, when the shoulder pushes it around to allow you to watch your shot.

It's trying to watch the shot, of course, which makes most beginners move their heads. They move it to the right in the backswing because they have not learned, physically, to control sway, and they move it to the left in the downswing because they cannot control, mentally, the urge to have a peek at the flight of the ball.

And this brings us to the second reason for not moving your head: If you lift your head by even the smallest fraction, it's still enough to lift your whole body off the shot.

And it's the damnedest bad habit to break.

Is there anything so frustrating as to be out on the course with a helpful friend who says, after every duffed shot you make, "You lifted your head again," when you are screaming silently to yourself, "I am *not* lifting my head!"

It's a tricky thing to learn, I guess, but the sorry fact is that you *are* lifting it. You may feel that you are concentrating like crazy to keep your head down, but in that last half-second of your downswing your concentration deserts you for a period so brief that it's almost too tiny to measure—but it's enough to bring your body completely off the shot, and you fail to make solid contact with the ball.

All I can do to help you here is to remind you that it's that old maxim again: The stroke is everything, the hitting of the ball is incidental. If you concentrate on achieving the proper stroke, you won't lift your head. If you lose concentration and either lunge at the ball, or experience that split second of panic that tells you that you've loused up something, you're odds-on to try to lift your head to check the damage.

Lifting your head, then, is largely a matter of lack of confidence. And that's a murderous deficiency in golf. You can't concentrate if you're not confident. You can't get your muscles to relax. You can't do one thing properly if your brain allows even the smallest doubt to seep in.

As far as moving the head is concerned, to tell you the truth I don't know whether I move mine or not, and I don't think it matters much. Because I know that when I concentrate on a smooth stroke in which I achieve maximum clubhead speed at that point on the grass where the ball is lying, and when I am confident that my stroke is going to make the ball go where it should—well, that's what happens. But as soon as I let other thoughts enter my mind, such as, "Oh, boy, I have to hit this one hard because I don't think I've got enough club," chances are I will jerk up my head a little to see if my fear was well founded.

Sure it throws the shot off. And it happens to everybody once in a while, because we're human and not machines. That's why a good golf shot gives you such a great sense of achievement: For a few split seconds you have turned a frail collection of bones and nerves and muscles into a precision instrument. It's some neat trick—and the best insurance to pull it off is to concentrate on the stroke and forget everything else, including the ball.

Before we leave this chapter, one last note. It's a funny thing about instruction, but no two people ever take it the same way. One man pays it casual lip service, another follows it with slavish step-by-step obedience.

Take the pause at the top of the backswing. I have avoided mentioning it up to now because some beginners—having been told that there should be a pause—lay too much stress on it and get no real value from it.

Its function is not particularly mysterious. It's that moment between when your wrists have cocked as much as they are able, and when your hips are able to overcome all the momentum of the backswing and start to come around in the downswing. It's the split second in which the flow reverses itself—but as to how big a split of one second it is . . . who knows?

But a friend of mine, firmly instructed that there should be a pause, figures that if it's worth recognizing at all, it should be recognized for all it's worth.

He has also been taught that his backswing should be slow, and his attitude on this is that the longer he can stretch out the backswing, the better. So there he is, a symphony of slow motion. It takes him forever to get up to the top of the backswing. And when he reaches it, he remains motionless. And remains, and remains, and remains. And at last he brings his club down—and actually gets off not-too-bad slugs of 150 yards or so.

Anyway, this stately style of his gets a lot of kidding. Once, after observing this frozen-statue technique for several shots, one member of the foursome said, "Aubrey, it's about your pause, the way you hold it so long. Just what are you doing up there?"

To which he solemnly replied, "I am praying."

"Oh," the other fellow said, "I thought you were waiting for an answer.

SUMMARY

1. Never try to hit the ball as hard as you can. By saving a little something, you're buying a little extra smoothness, which will make the ball go further in the long run.

2. In the first 12 inches of take-away you should be able (out of the corner of your eye) to see the clubhead begin to curve inside the intended line of flight. If you can't see it by then, it's unlikely it's going to happen later—which means you'll be hitting outside-in—and that means a slice.

3. Every once in a while, stop at the top of the backswing and try to turn the toe of your club toward the sky. It's a good check to see if you're keeping your clubface square throughout the swing (toe up, clubhead square; toe down or back, clubhead open). Your left hand should be on top of the shaft at the top of the backswing, and your right hand should be under the shaft.
4. Don't try to cure a slice by aiming left or toeing in the clubhead. Correct your grip and your swing, not the course or the equipment.
5. Don't try to get the shaft parallel to the ground at the top of the backswing *at the expense of the proper grip*. An over-swing is much worse than a slightly shortened backswing.
6. Strive to achieve a late hit, by getting all of your body through the shot before the clubhead gets there. It should help to practice aiming the butt of the shaft at the ball as long as you can in the downswing.
7. Keep your head steady—but not rigid—over the ball. The shoulders turn under the chin, while the chin remains as stationary as possible.
8. Don't try to swing while you're still worried about something else. Confidence is required in concentration, and concentration is required in every shot.

What's So Tough About Bogey?

Among the touring pros there's an old saying: "Drive for show, putt for dough."

Most of the rest of us know the saying, but the difference between the duffer and the pro is that the pro abides by it. Our whole short game gets less attention than we devote to a single club, the No. 1 wood. All we have in our heads is this obsession to whack the ball out of sight.

Okay, but let's suppose you can't. Let's suppose that you have some kind of hangup which absolutely limits your longest drive to 150 yards. But let us also suppose that you can do everything else properly. When you drive 150 yards, it is dead straight. When you chip, the ball goes in the exact direction and to the exact distance you intended. And when you pick up your putter, you need it no more than 36 times over 18 greens. (Which is hardly putting for dough; with a little instruction and a lot of practice, anybody should be able to average better than two putts per green over a whole round, a point we will discuss fully a little later on.)

Anyway, so here you are, poor fellow, with a governor on your long game which limits you to 150 yards, but with all the rest of your game in good shape. What sort of score do you think you would turn in with this dreadful handicap?

By now, you can guess what's coming. With even this apparently limited artillery, I doubt if there are half a dozen golf courses in all of North America so tough that you couldn't tour them in a stroke or less than 90. In other words, bogey golf or better.

Oh, sure, there's the occasional hole that defies this rule. Take the eighteenth at Tulsa's Southern Hills, site of the 1970 P.G.A. It's a par 4, and for the pros it played to 458 yards. That in itself is tough enough, but this super hole has a dog-leg right which requires a 240- to 245-yard drive to reach—leaving only a trifling 200-yard-plus second shot to the green. No sense kidding you; you ain't going to handle this baby in bogey, poking it only 150 yards. In fact Tommy Bolt, who won the 1958 Open at Southern Hills, got par on this monster only once in four rounds, bogeyed it twice, and had to take a double bogey on the second day.

The point is, duffers almost never see holes like this. The tees are set way back for tournament play, then way forward every other day of the year.

So let's take a more standard configuration and see how it would play for the 150-yard shooter. Let's say it's a par 5, 540 yards, crescent-shaped to the right, with all kinds of playing surface on the left, but with a solid forest which extends from the tee to the cup on your slicing side. (This is a common par-5 layout, and I have picked it because you have probably played a similar hole yourself.)

As we have said, your long shot is 150 yards—and you can probably reach it with not only your driver, but with all the clubs down to about the 3 iron. It's quite common for high handicappers to hit almost exactly the same distance with several clubs, even though the competent golfer expects to get about ten yards further with each successively longer weapon. What seems to happen to the beginner is that he hits less confidently with the ultimate distance weapon—the driver—but has at least one fairway club which doesn't frighten him, and he gets as far with it as he does with the No. 1 wood. Let's suppose in this case it's your 3 iron, and you have remembered the rule that the golf course is no place to try to correct club problems. In an actual game, play competitively, not experimentally—therefore leave the dubious wood in the bag and go with the confident iron.

So here you are at the tee, 3 iron in hand, with 540 yards to conquer in no more than six strokes. A piece of cake. Tee shot, 150 yards; second shot, another 150; third, another 150; a 90-yard approach to the green, two putts, and you've got a bogey 6.

As far as bogey is concerned, so much for the long hit.

Oh, come on now, you say. If I were playing that hole in a test tube, I might do it in bogey—but what about the guy who can hit only 150 yards and can't count on doing anything else right, either?

All right, then. Let us play this hole with everything we have learned up to now, and see if we can still scramble a bogey out of it.

Our first requirement is a game plan (Chapter Three). With only 150 yards per stroke going for us, it is going to take four strokes to reach a green 540 yards away. The trouble is a solid wall of trees on the right. If we land in those trees *once*, and have to use at least a stroke to get out, we no longer have enough fairway strokes left to reach the green in four.

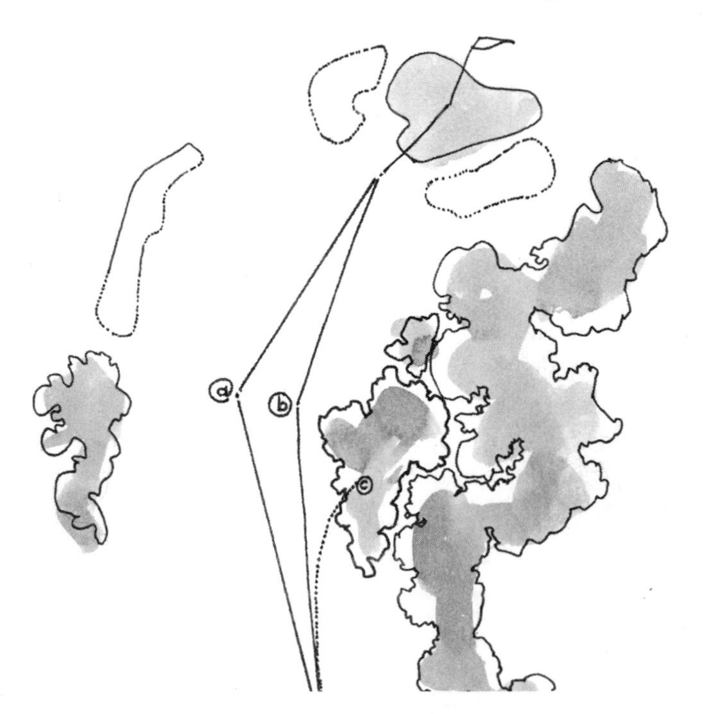

HOW WOULD YOU PLAY THIS HOLE? It's 540 yards, par 5, dogleg right—which is where all the trouble is. The expert would take Line B, shaving the corner to save yards. Reckless duffers try this, too—but even a slight slice means Line C and a trip in the woods. Line A is the beginner's choice, because keeping the ball in play is what it's all about.

Therefore, our game starts to take shape in the form of the question (Chapter Five):

How do I have to play this stroke to make absolutely sure the ball will be kept in play?

If we do not have this burning question in mind, what are the alternatives? Well, of course, we could just step up to the ball and give it a lash (which certainly I have done in thousands of situations in the past to no good result). The trouble with this procedure is that, with no game plan in mind, whatever happens—good or bad—is pure, mindless luck, Russian roulette with a golf club. Or we could try that cunning little number of attempting to sneak around the crescent, shaving as close to the right-side trees as possible, and thereby reduce the yardage to the green. It has only two drawbacks: It's dead dangerous, and it's unnecessary. Four strokes, we have already determined, is plenty to reach the green with 60 yards to spare. Any plan which could add a stroke, whatever its other advantages, just isn't worth it.

So, having decided properly that staying out of trouble is the plan, you aim for the safe, fat part of the fairway which gives you the widest berth from trouble in case anything

goes wrong. Having selected your target area, you follow the lining-up procedure which will bring your feet parallel to the desired line of flight (Chapter Five). You carefully assume the grip which will provide the best insurance of meeting the ball squarely (Chapter Four), and you give that grip the best insurance to do its stuff with a smooth, unhurried swing (Chapter Eight).

At this point, the reader has to take over. I don't know where your ball landed because I've never seen you play. If you're still in the process of putting it all together, and a couple of points are still a little slow in coming, this hypothetical tee shot may not have happened quite as you wanted. But out of all the things which affect a golf shot, let us assume that you now have enough of them at your command that your shot carried 150 yards and stayed on the fairway well enough placed that it has not set up a problem for your second shot. When you reach your ball, you find it is sitting up on the turf in a good lie, it has landed on a flat portion of the fairway—demanding no expertise in up- or down- or side-hill lies, which we haven't talked about yet—and you can clearly see a good landing area for your second stroke.

Great. Do everything all over again, and give it another stroke.

Ooops! This time, in spite of all your good intentions, something goes wrong. You met the ball all right, and it went its 150 yards, but a little bit of slice sneaked in somehow, and it came back over to the right, landing only five feet from the woods. Two problems arise. First of all, you're not sure what you did wrong, so you can't be sure you can eliminate the mistake in the next shot. Second, although the ball has covered 300 yards in two strokes, the loss to lateral movement has reduced the forward distance carried to only 285 yards.

You are still, therefore, 255 yards from the green, tight to the crescent of trees, and somewhat stymied by them.

Now what do you do?

Any touring pro worth his card would step out to the middle of the fairway, estimate the distance and the angle, then step up to his ball, set himself up for a fade around the partial stymie of the trees, and go for the green.

And the duffer? It is uncanny, it is mind-boggling, and it is downright ridiculous—but at this point the average high-handicap golfer nine times out of ten will try exactly the same thing. He will try to fade a shot around a bulge of trees to a green so far away he couldn't hit it with a cannon. Or, if this is not precisely what he is trying to do, he is most certainly not asking himself that vital game-plan question: What do I do now to make certain that this ball will remain in play?

If you ask yourself that question, there is only one answer. Originally, you were willing to accept that this hole would require four shots to reach the green. You have used up two of them, and have turned up the pressure slightly by having lost 15 yards of forward distance to lateral waste. But with only 255 yards to go, you still have the capability of reaching the green with your next two strokes—providing your third stroke travels at least 105 yards toward the pin *and stays in play*.

That's your answer: Look for a place to land the ball which is well away from the forest you are almost in, and which will bring you within putting-surface range when you take your fourth shot.

Ironically, your tendency toward the unexpected slice can now work for you. It isn't controllable enough that you can risk skimming around the trees, because it may carry on right into them. But if you play to the fat part of the fairway now (obviously with a club which will keep you short of drilling into the left side if you hit it straight), even a fairly strong slice will tend to leave you in a great position in mid-fairway.

But let's stop for a moment and recap what's happened. If you were to take a hurried, ill-considered third shot and land in the trees, and it then took you a poke or two to get onto the fairway again, another to finally get onto the green, and two putts to get down, your potential bogey 6 would have become at least a 7 and maybe an 8. And if you were asked which shot caused the double or triple bogey, what would your answer be?

Most duffers would say it was the third shot, the one which landed in the jungle. Or they might even blame their high score on the poor recovery from the jungle. Yet obviously the second shot was the culprit. If it hadn't landed on the edge of the woods, partially stymied, there would have been no need for the hurried, ill-considered third shot. If Number Two had gone a straight 150 yards, Number Three would have been a routine duplication of it.

So what am I getting at? Just this: If you don't recognize the culprit shot, you don't always realize when you're in danger. And if you don't realize your danger, you're liable to try something that will land you squarely in trouble. All too often, when a man lands in danger, you'll hear his partner say something like, "How is it, can you get at it?" as if simply being able to hit the ball will solve everything. Obviously, in this case it won't solve everything. If you could almost get into the woods from the middle of the fairway on the second shot, you have a damn sight better chance of landing there when playing from only five feet away. Being able to hit it is no real consolation *unless you can hit it out of trouble and get back on your game plan at the same time.*

Thus, we're right back to the need for Realistic Assessment, which we first considered way back in Chapter One. If you are not constantly putting it to work, you are inviting those 8s and 9s with which your scorecard is all too frequently decorated.

Whenever you score anything higher than double bogey, the culprit is not only the initial poor stroke, but your lack of mental alertness. I say "double bogey" rather than merely one over, because it is only being realistic to concede that there are some situations which may call for unexpected extra strokes per round.

If your ball lands in a bad divot, say, it is reasonable to assume that you are not skilled enough to get the full value of the recovery from the divot which you would normally expect from a good grassy lie. Or, if you find yourself on the green as the result of a good shot, but you're still 80 feet from the pin, you can be putting fairly well and still need three strokes to get it down. Or, on a really long par 4 you can easily use up one shot for distance and another on direction, and score a double bogey 6 without having played badly.

But whenever your score is higher than double bogey, you are likely to be kidding yourself if you blame it on bad luck or your lack of physical competence or skill. Your trouble is in your head.

Which, of course, is the last area in which any of us are keen to accept advice or criticism. Yet all of us play dumbly occasionally. And all of us know it, too. We admit it all the time. The split second after the shot has gone wrong, we say, "Yeah, I knew I shouldn't have played it that way."

It's a matter of degree, really. As members of a race of nonsupermen, we're going to occasionally play dumbly no matter how much we try not to. The trick is to find out whether we are personally exceeding the national average.

Next time you're out on the course, why not try this, just to see how much mental paralysis is affecting your game:

On one side of your scorecard mark the number of strokes lost to par which you honestly think were the result of lack of physical skill or lack of knowledge as to how a shot should be played. On the other side of the card mark down all those strokes lost because of mental lapse, whether it occurred on the green, on the fairway, or on the tee.

In the hole we have been playing hypothetically, for instance, I would say that the second shot, which landed you within five feet of the woods, was a result of lack of physical skill or lack of knowledge. You were trying to do everything right, and it happened to go wrong. But the attempt to skim around the trees on the third stroke showed a lack of realistic assessment. Chalk one stroke to playing skills, and the other to mental lapse.

At the end of the round, add up both sets of figures. The first set represents the work that lies ahead of you in developing a good stroke. The second set is what keeps you from shooting bogey golf.

The point I am making is that bogey is not tough. It doesn't demand one skill or physical attribute beyond the reach of the average middle-aged, sedentary, fat-beamed office drudge. And it comes infinitely more easily if you get into some sort of shape.

That's another sensitive area for most people. We don't like being told that we're not using our heads, and we don't like to face the dread prospect of (ugh!) getting into physical condition.

Sometimes it really is incredible what we expect to achieve for nothing. Why shouldn't you be quivering in the leg muscles after hauling a golf cart up hill and down dale for four miles—if the only physical preparation you have brought to it is sliding behind the wheel of your car? Or why wouldn't you pull a back muscle which has hitherto seen active duty only while helping to raise your finger to signal the waiter?

To play good golf, you don't have to be able to leap tall buildings at a single bound, but you shouldn't stumble crossing a deep pile rug, either.

To play good golf, you have to be able to walk without getting tired, you have to be able to stretch leg and back and arm muscles without danger, and it doesn't do any harm to build up strength in your hands and wrists and forearms.

My own fitness program started with walking. I hated it. But I also hated puffing like a whale trying to reach an elevated green. So I started walking to the corner store for cigarettes. Then I began walking to work, taking a cab at whatever point my finely tuned body announced quits.

First thing I knew I was walking to work and back. Then I was walking simply for walking's sake. And then I noticed my pants didn't fit any more, so wasted was my combination belly and bumper guard. Old ladies stopped assisting me across the street. Young ones stopped calling me "sir."

Then I started a modest exercise program seriously. Apart from the walking, it takes about five minutes a day. It's a modification of the now famous Royal Canadian Air Force 5BX (Five Basic Exercises), and if you'd like to try it, I can assure you that in three months, at five minutes a day plus a long walk, the most out-of-shape guy in the world will be fit enough to play 36 holes of golf.

All you need is a clock or watch with a second hand, and two tennis balls.

Each exercise is exactly 60 seconds. Increase the number of exercises you can cram into a minute only as your body dictates. As your condition improves, your number or "reps" will increase with it.

1. This is a stretching exercise. Bend over and attempt to touch your toes. If you can't reach your toes, don't worry about it but consider just how out of elastic condition you are; but suppleness will come. Keep it up for exactly one minute and go on to the next exercise.
2. Lie on your back with your fingers laced behind your head and sit up without raising your heels from the floor. Or rather, try to. It'll come, it'll come. Another 60 seconds.
3. Still on your back, put your hands at your sides and raise your legs, knees straight, about 12 inches. Lower very slowly. Do this for 60 seconds.
4. Roll over and do push-ups for 60 seconds. Well, what about push-up, singular?
5. Grip a tennis ball in each fist, and squeeze and release for 60 seconds.

If I can't convince you to try walking, how about running on the spot? Try it for two minutes, as Exercise 6, and aim to get a high knee lift.

With all of these exercises, don't try for speed particularly, but rather, try to go at a rate which will call for some real determination to complete the last 15 seconds. It's that one minute and that last 15 seconds of effort which make the whole program pay off in good overall conditioning and body-building for golf, so you can develop the stamina, strength, and elasticity which make a round really enjoyable.

Meanwhile, back at the course, we have taken three shots which have brought us 450 yards along the fairway, and all that remains to bring us bogey is to get the ball into the cup in the next three shots. With the problems of the fairway behind us, we are halfway home. "Except," you may now be saying, "for the little problem of my not being able to approach or putt, either."

Well, if this be true, there is no human way you will ever shoot bogey, so we had best proceed to the next chapter and get to work on your short game.

SUMMARY

1. Get your definitions straight. When you're in trouble you're in the rough, or the trap, or the water; when you're in danger, those are the places you're going to be in if your present shot goes wrong. Recognize a dangerous lie when you get to it, and then head for safety before you get into more trouble.
2. Use your scorecard to keep a three-way running check on your game: how many strokes you've played, how many strokes you've lost through inexperience, and how many strokes you've lost because you didn't think. It may take you a whole season to stop slicing, but you could stop making bad decisions today, if you tried.
3. Spend five minutes a day on getting in physical shape for golf. You'll feel better, you'll live longer, and it will speed up the time it takes to get your game in shape.

Those Last Few Yards to Glory

I think the average high-handicap golfer would do himself a big favor if he could learn to think of every hole as a two-part problem, and get it thoroughly into his head that the bigger part of the problem comes last.

Usually, we do it the other way around. Our major concern is the tee shot. If only we can blast it 250 yards off the tee, all will be well.

Take the par 5 we've been discussing. Suppose this was an actual hole you were playing and you got off a superb tee shot, 220 yards right down the middle. Then you haul out the 3 wood and crack out a beautiful fairway shot for another 200 yards. Then, from 100 yards out, you spend five shots getting the ball into the cup, and your score for the hole is a double bogey 7.

Would you be displeased with your performance? I'll bet not. I'll bet 99 duffers out of 100 would march to the next hole savoring the memory of the two splendid fairway pokes—and discreetly draw a curtain over their performance in the really big part of the problem—getting a 1.68-inch ball into a 4.25-inch hole in the ground in the lowest possible number of strokes.

No doubt about it, it really is a great feeling to watch your drive zoom off the tee. And it's enough to make you part with your lunch when it only dribbles off.

But either way, it's still only one stroke.

And call me a heretic if you will, but it's not the most important stroke. A good second shot can go a long way toward recovering from a poor tee shot. A good golfer who has spent some time and effort learning how to scramble can get into a whale of a lot of trouble on the fairway and still walk away from the hole more or less intact. But the man with limited skills in the short game can be super off the tee all day and still be a pigeon for the man who shines when he gets in close.

I'm not telling you anything new, of course. We all know the hard facts. But because the good long shots are so damned pretty, we all tend to overemphasize their importance.

Viewed in the cold light of golfing realism, however, they are nothing more than Part One of a two-part problem; they get us into a position where the men are separated from the boys.

Part Two of the problem begins when we reach that point on every hole where the club we are holding could put the ball in the cup—and its minimum duty is to get the ball close enough so that the next shot definitely should make it drop.

It's particularly important for the duffer to develop a good short game because he spends so much time just off the green. More often than not, the high handicapper almost never gets on in regulation. The low handicapper may never use his wedge or 9 iron; the high handicapper may use it 20 or 30 times.

That's a bit of a shocker, isn't it? Most of us devote hours of practice to the slammer and next to nothing on the finesse stick, although it gets twice as much use in an actual game.

So let's give the power weapons a rest, and consider the approach clubs. Which ones are they?

The way it works out for me is that all clubs from the wedge down to the 7 iron are approach equipment. The reason for that is that I can hit the 6 iron about 150 yards, but from that distance I am not reliable enough to be able to count on landing on the green. So it's still a fairway weapon. Its principal function is still to cover ground in a more or less straight line. However, when I get within 7-iron range or closer, I am no longer concerned with covering ground, but with landing in a precise spot.

What's the point of making the distinction? It's another step in that continuing process of breaking up each hole into a series of separate problems. Whenever I pick up the 7, 8, 9, or wedge, I am putting the pressure on myself to accept that the fairway phase of the problem is behind me, and I am now going right for the cup. No kidding myself that the shot is only supposed to get me close to the green—it's supposed to get me right to the flag.

If you have never thought about your higher-lofted clubs this way, it's a good idea to start. We waste so many strokes by playing patty-cake, by not realizing that This Is It. We wait until we're five feet from the hole before we really start to think seriously about making the ball drop into it.

Another way to think about your approach clubs is that they have more power than you're going to ask of them. In other words, when you use them, you will tend to purposely over-club yourself.

I'll admit, the pros don't often do this, because their stroke is so smooth that they can tell you within a very few yards just how far each shot is going to go. But the beginner can't do that. He's erratic, getting a different distance every time he uses the club. That's because his swing isn't smooth. He's trying too hard. Overreaching.

So why not remove that hazard by purposely choosing a club which will more than do the job. Forget about trying to make the ball go as far as you hit it last Thursday, and concentrate on making it go a precise distance which is well within the range of your worst shot. Then you can abbreviate your swing and go for smoothness, rather than peak power. Needless to say, smooth shots go straighter, too.

This raises a point we have not touched on up to this

point, and yet it is mandatory for every shot, whether it be your drive or your approach or your putt. And that is the practice stroke.

I consider it particularly necessary in the case of the approach and the putt. You can frequently recover from the effects of a bad drive, but once it gets down to the crunch and you are aiming for the pin, the chips are down and every mis-hit adds another stroke to the hole.

Therefore, the practice stroke is terribly important. But what a waste of time it can be if you don't know why you're doing it.

Agreed, when you're standing at the first tee, you can get good use out of a really lusty practice cut if it's part of your overall warm-up. Loosens the muscles, etc.

But what about those guys all of us have seen, flailing away with furious energy, even though the shot they are preparing for is only a 20-yard chip.

What in the world is the point of whacking the hell out of thin air? All it does is tire you out.

The practice swing in the approach situation is meant to accomplish two objectives. First, it gives you the feel of the club. Even though the driver and the 9-iron strokes are essentially the same, there is obviously a great deal of difference in the clubs themselves. You take the practice swing to reacquaint your mind and your body with the distinctive characteristics of each club.

And I don't think you can say you've got the feel of the club until you can give it a practice stroke which trims the grass. That's where your ball is, right on the deck, so there's no point stepping up to it if all you've done in your practice stroke is swish the air around.

Many beginning golfers have an unconscious reluctance to trim the grass. They are afraid they will take a divot and invite the displeasure of the course superintendent. This is a difficult notion to shake, because it is part of our innate good manners concerning other people's property. But the course superintendent will not jump you for taking a divot—only for not replacing it.

Feel guilty about taking a divot? Relax, you're on a golf course, not somebody's lawn. Taking divots is part of golf (as long as you put them back!).

Another reason some people don't like to trim the grass is that they can't. They become stricken with what I suppose you could call "anticipatory panic." It used to happen to me all the time. I was so convinced that I was going to ruin the shot that I didn't like to take a serious practice swing because I didn't like the early warning it was giving me. I would get so panicky, I was literally incapable of getting the clubhead down to ground level. After a couple of attempts I would give up, step up to the ball, and hope that what I couldn't make happen in practice would magically happen in the crunch. Don't build your dream castle on that hope.

The problem is nerves. You don't know how to make the shot anyway, so you're pretend-practicing. Because you're pretend-practicing, you're not concentrating on anything, so you're lifting your head. Which, as we now know, lifts your body, which lifts your arms and hands, which lifts the club, which makes you top the ball.

I must admit I still do it occasionally. But now I make it work for me. If I fail to trim the grass on a practice stroke now, I say, ah-ha, you rascal, you're not concentrating!

But how can the poor duffer concentrate if he doesn't really know what he's trying to do?

Which brings us to the second objective of the practice stroke, which is to tell you the amount of beef required to put the ball up to the pin—and, for that matter, into the hole. (After all, it's got to go in there sometime, so why not right now? Think positive and try hard. Occasionally it really will go in.)

There's no way anyone else can tell you exactly how much steam to put on a shot. The only thing you do know is that it can't be 100 percent, because you've already over-clubbed yourself—and certainly you've over-clubbed yourself whenever you're within 50 yards or so—so obviously an all-out hit would put you over the green.

The extent to which you shorten your swing is a matter of practice, and some indefinable ability within us all which somehow senses what the correct weight should be.

That may sound pretty vague, but let me remind you that the principle of target image does work.

I have found that consistent results can be achieved by using the following system:

Take a practice swing to get the feel of the club. Keep at it until there is a definite sensation of clubhead weight, and until the clubhead is trimming the grass.

Then line up a couple of feet from the ball and take a good look at the target. Then, with an image of the target in your mind, take a practice swing which you think would be strong enough to put the ball there. Then trust your senses. If they suggest you were too light or too heavy, practice-swing until the weight seems right. Then hit the ball.

That's the general principle. Now let's take it apart in detail.

I try to assess the target from two points of view. First, I try to estimate its exact yardage; then I look at it in relation to shots I have made in the past with the same club. I know, for instance, that I'm good for a smooth 110 yards with a 9 iron. Beyond that, I risk pushing it. If I look at a target and I estimate it's between 120 and 125 yards away, even if it appears to be about the same distance as I have previously achieved with the 9 iron, I'll think about it a bit more.

What's happening is that I've got two sets of facts at odds with each other, and I'd like them to get together. Either that target is really 125 yards away, and I'd have to push a 9 iron to get there, or it's really a comfortable 9-iron shot and therefore it must only be 110 yards away. If those two sets of facts refuse to mesh, my tendency is to go down to a 7 iron, knowing I've got too much club, and shorten my swing a little.

You'll get a lot of argument about this bit of advice, and I have considered the various arguments before giving it to you, but I still think I'm right. Look at it this way. If you approach a shot with any doubt in your mind as to whether you've got enough club, it's going to distract you at least a little bit. Even if it was exactly the right club to use, that little bit of doubt could make you play it badly. But if you know perfectly well you've got too much club, and by taking practice swings you're able to make the necessary adjustment, I don't see that you can go very far wrong.

Duffers almost always land short of the hole. The worst that could happen with over-clubbing and holding back a little is that you could go a bit long—but you can also hit the stick going long, and plop it right into the cup. And there's no way you can do that if you're short.

Now, as for the shot itself, there's no difference between the finesse stroke and the distance stroke except the backswing. You don't want to go quite as far back because you don't want all the distance the club can give you. As for your follow-through, as far as you're concerned it's exactly the same as with the distance stroke. Actually, it will foreshorten because there's not as much momentum in the stroke, but *never* try to deliberately foreshorten it.

If you try to shorten up on follow-through, you are certain to pull up *not* in the follow-through, but *before* you hit the ball. The combination of the shortened backswing and the pull-up will make you tear out your hair because you'll only go half the distance you wanted to go.

It is of paramount importance that you don't try to hit the ball softly. It must be stroked just as crisply as the tee shot. If you try purposely to be gentle with it, you will unconsciously try to scoop it up and the best you can hope for is a little bloop into the air.

Also very important: Keep in mind that even the short shots are golf shots. All the usual rules apply: Shove the clubhead back, don't lift it up; keep the left arm straight; initiate the downswing with the hips. When it's a finesse shot, any breakdown in the swing is disastrous.

This warning is particularly important when you are only a few yards—let's say 20 or so—from the putting surface.

Don't try to baby the ball onto the green, it almost never works. Keep in mind that every shot is a golf shot, no matter how short a distance you want it to travel. It has a backswing, a downswing, an impact, and follow-through. Practice until you get the feel of how much or little of these elements is going to be required, and then forget about how "delicate" it is, and just step up and do it.

At this point, the duffer is under a tremendous temptation to try to hit the ball *softly* with his hands, to try to *deposit* it on the green, rather than *stroke* it here. He is also under tremendous pressure to lift his head to watch the shot.

Tension is the deadly enemy of the short approach shot. I think it comes mostly from the fact that it's such a little stroke. There's so little body movement to relieve the tension.

So I do the opposite of what all the good instruction books suggest. They say, quite properly, that there's almost no body movement in the short approach; it's all wrists and hands. But trying to keep by body still and use only my wrists and hands gets me twitchy. So I practice-swing with a stroke which has a modest little knee-hip-shoulder turn and then systematically cut it down. I find I can't start off with a hands-and-wrists-only shot, but I can back into it.

Here are some points to keep in mind during the practice:

If the ball is going to pop into the air with enough backspin to stop it quickly, you must hit down and through the ball. Therefore you must have your weight slightly ahead of the ball (favoring the left foot), and the bottom point of your arc must be under the ball. This means that you will encounter the turf. Make sure you get used to the shock of hitting the turf, or you're almost sure to stub the shot and not follow through—thereby getting an unexpected punch shot which could send your ball right off the green. In the course of getting used to the shock of encountering the turf, adjust the pressure of your grip so that the sudden resistance doesn't allow the clubshaft to turn in your fingers. Also, remember that the shorter the shot, the shorter the backswing; therefore the weight of the clubhead will do very little in the way of helping you cock your wrists. You have to cock them early yourself, so that you get a nice, strong sensation of clubhead weight even though your backswing only travels 30 to 40 inches. Finally, keep your stance slightly open—right foot forward, left foot back—so that your left hip is already out of your way when you come down into the shot.

Once you get the hang of it, it's a lovely feeling to execute a neat little chip. All of the basic tempo and timing of the golf shot are in the chip, and the full power stroke with your driver is merely an extension of it.

A point that may help in gauging your distance: Some golfers find they have a limited natural ability in judging the amount of beef required in the short game, but all of us can pick up a stone or baseball and lob it into a 10-foot ring from 20, 30, or 40 yards away with no trouble at all. Within a yard or two, it takes about the same amount of effort to pitch a golf ball onto a green with a club as it takes to lob a baseball with an underhand throw. Or if this isn't precisely true, it feels as if it is. Which is what you're looking for: A physical sensation which will reliably indicate the amount of power the approach shot requires.

As for your choice of landing areas on the green, that depends upon how good you are at stopping your ball. Most high-handicap golfers simply can't make their ball bite—and until you can shoot regularly in the mid-90s, I think you have enough to work on without worrying about this deficiency. But in the meantime you've got to take it into account. You shouldn't aim to land right beside the pin on first bounce if you know your ball is going to keep on rolling another 25 feet.

So here's my suggestion: Whenever you are close enough to the green so that you have a chance to actually aim at a precise landing spot, try to hit 20 feet short of the cup. From there it should roll no more than 10 feet past. If the flag is placed only 20 feet from the front of the green, cut the distance in half and aim for the 10-foot position.

But always aim for the putting surface when the flag is placed tight. You'll probably go further past the pin than you'd like, but it beats landing on the fairway, which can give some very weird bounces. Or even worse, the ball could plug itself, if it's just been raining—and if it plugs itself on the fairway, you can't unplug it, which you legally can on the putting surface.

What club do you use for the short approach? From 15 yards out, up to its comfortable limit, go with your wedge or your highest-lofted club, and aim as I have suggested above. At any distance closer than 15 yards, go with whatever weapon will give you enough flight to land you on the putting surface halfway to the stick. Don't try to scoop the ball. Hit it crisply, and expect that it will go low and roll the rest of the way to the pin.

What happens if fortune refuses to smile on you, and your ball lands in a sand trap?

Well, at least you can take heart from the fact that everybody does it, and everybody has trouble when it happens. The pro's trouble is different from yours, but it's still trouble.

The duffer's problem is that it's extremely difficult to get sand trap practice. I've never seen a practice trap at a driving range or a pay-as-you-play course, and I've seen very few on private courses.

How are you ever to learn, then, how to handle the beach? By trial and error, I suppose, which is the way most golfers learned it. You get into a trap and you try to remember the basic rules about getting out.

And that's the first rule: to get out. Forget about "making the shot" unless your ball is well set up and you can get good footing.

The second rule is to understand the problem. What is so different about a sand trap? Why is it difficult to get out of?

Because sand is tougher to negotiate than grass. You can't send your clubhead through the sand and under the ball with the same ease that you can pick it off the turf.

The solution, then, would seem to be to develop a club which would help overcome this problem, and of course, that's what the wedge is. It has a sharp leading edge which bites into the sand with a minimum amount of drag, and a heavy, bulged-out sole with prohibits the club from biting too deeply. A rather ingenious club design: a biting edge to get you under the ball, a bulged-out sole to stop you from getting too far under.

All you have to know now is how to put it to work.

The same old principle applies, namely that the exit from the sand trap is essentially a golf shot. First, you wiggle your feet into the sand until you've got a good, firm footing—which, since it's against the rules to ground your club, also gives you a tip as to the consistency of the stuff—then you aim at a spot about an inch or two behind the ball. And then you execute a normal stroke—which means you swing crisply, positively, down and through the ball, and up and out into the follow-through.

Where's all the difficulty then? How come the duffer so often goes wrong in the trap?

First of all, by psyching himself that he's got more of a problem than really exists. He gets nervous and twitchy and doesn't keep his head down. He stabs at the ball. And he doesn't follow through. And as often as not, even though he has hit *at* it very hard, the ball barely moves.

The key is the follow-through. In a properly executed shot the clubhead enters the sand just behind the ball, still moving on a downward path. It then lifts the ball *and the sand*—not because the golfer tries to lift anything, but because both the ball and the sand are perched on the clubface as the clubface itself is lifted as a natural part of the follow-through. If you don't follow through, all you do is give the sand a wallop and the ball is barely disturbed.

Confidence in the shot comes from knowing what's got to happen, that the ball has to be lifted out of the trap on a bed of sand.

The problem is in two parts, the aim and the swing.

If you dig in too far back of the ball, you may literally lack the strength to excavate enough sand to do the proper job of lifting. If you have aimed a mite too close, on the other hand, you may miss the sand entirely and give the ball a blade hit, sending it too far—like into the trap on the other side of the green.

Most high-handicap players err on the side of aiming too close. We have a strange urge to be fastidious, and we feel

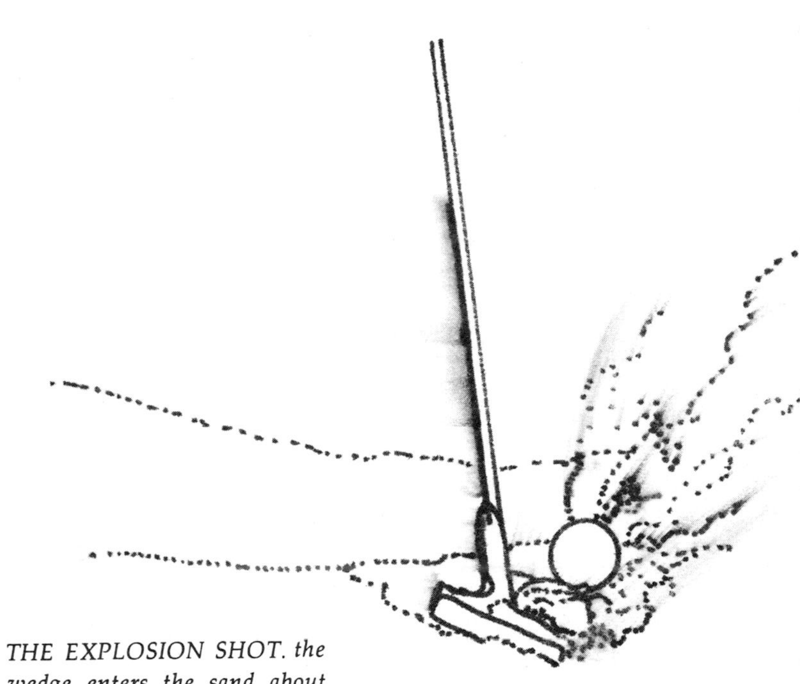

THE EXPLOSION SHOT. the wedge enters the sand about two inches behind the ball and then explodes a mound of sand into the air. The ball simply sits on top of that mound and gets carried along with it. The important thing is to follow through normally, otherwise there's no momentum to lift the ball and all you're doing is stirring sand.

it isn't quite nice to send a spray of sand all over the playing surface; so either we try to pick it clean, or we try to minimize the spray of sand by letting up on the follow-through. Neither solution is reliable.

It's better to aim a bit fat, say three inches behind the ball, and then hit down and through with lots of authority. Taking all that sand will stop the ball from going too far, and taking a full swing will ensure that you get out of the trap.

If it has been raining and the sand is fairly packed, your ball may not sink into it at all. It may be sitting up pretty as a picture. In such cases, I always go for the clean pick, figuring that the sand is so heavy that any miscalculation in the normal explosion shot will put me up against more resistance than I can handle.

Which means that I tend always to go for the shot which I think will be the *easiest* for me, the shot I'm most likely to make, rather than the one which will be superb if it works and a disaster if it doesn't. Further, if the surface of the bunker is smooth and firm and there's little or no lip to it, I don't hesitate to consider using my putter as the exit weapon. There may not be any classic beauty to the shot, but that sort of window dressing shouldn't even enter your mind. It's getting out of trouble that counts, not being fancy.

Once you do gain confidence in the matter of getting out, you're ready for the next step, which is going where you want to go. Since the shot requires very little body and a lot of hands and arms, it's a good idea to get your left hip out of the way at address, by taking an open stance. This means, though, that your swing will tend toward the outside-in flight path, and the ball will tend to go to the right. Aim a little left to compensate. Remember, too, that the shot is going to slow down considerably because of the drag of the sand. Therefore the stroke will have to be a little harder than the normal chip from the grass to carry the same distance. As with every other shot from in close, remind yourself that the ball will never drop in the cup if it never reaches it, so go right for the hole. Don't think of it as your last fairway shot; think of it as your first putt.

Do it right, and occasionally it will be your only putt.

SUMMARY

1. There's a big difference between going for the green and going for the cup. Go for the smaller target as soon as you can. Often the duffer will be well within range for a precision shot, and waste the opportunity by not recognizing it. He fails to hit the target because he failed to try.
2. Take a few practice swings before every shot, particularly before the precision shots: the approaches and the putts. You should be able to trim the grass in practice before you try to hit the ball. Don't try to hit it until you can.
3. Never try to hit the ball softly. Every shot in the repertoire must be crisp and authoritative.
4. When in doubt about distance, over-club yourself and swing easily, rather than trying to strain a few extra yards by overswinging.
5. Always be willing to go a shade long. According to the old saying, "If it's not up, it will never go in." Duffers are notorious for shooting short.
6. If you tend to tense up when faced with a delicate little chip, start your practice sequence by "hitting it too big," and then systematically reduce the swing to the right weight. The shorter the shot, the smoother it must be.
7. If you can't judge weight easily, imagine you're lobbing the ball underhand, then stroke it with what feels like the same amount of effort.
8. When you get in the sand, remember that the first requirement is to get out—any way you can.
9. Remember, the "explosion shot" from sand is exactly that, an explosion of sand caused by your club biting in a couple of inches behind the ball and then carrying through. It's the follow-through which makes it an explosion; otherwise it's just an earth tremor, and that won't get the ball out.

Happiness Is a One-Putt Green

I don't know whether good putters are born or if they're made. But I do know that anybody can be a better putter with a little practice.

Of all the requirements the duffer needs to turn himself into a competent putter, the first and foremost is Confidence.

It is absolutely essential that you assume your putt is going to drop if you are within 25 feet of the cup. Because it is also absolutely essential that your stroke from 25 feet be so close to dropping in that your next putt is only a tap-in.

If you say to yourself, and to everybody else, "Well, I'll just lag this one up," you may think you are providing yourself with an excuse if you fail to drop it, but what you are really doing is setting up a three-putt situation—one to get you in range, one to really try, and one to really drop the ball.

You must be confident that you can make the first putt, even from as far as 25 feet—because illogical confidence must overcome logical distrust. If you were to use logic only, you would never believe that any putt beyond about two feet could be made.

Let's look at the long putt from the point of view of logic. Put three golf balls side by side, touching each other, and assume that the middle one is positioned right over the center of the cup. Obviously it's in a perfect line to drop in. The other two, a half-ball width off line, would also drop but they would fall off the side of the cup to do it. Move over one more ball-width, however, and you miss the cup. That's how small the target is.

And logic tells you that a free-standing man, operating by sight and feel alone, has almost no chance of finding that small a target from anything more than point-blank range.

Yet we do it all the time. We're like a bumblebee who doesn't know that it's physically impossible for him to fly, so he just flies anyway.

What we need in putting is bumblebee confidence.

I walk onto a green thinking as positively as I can. "Damn," I say to myself, "I have taken four strokes just to get on the green; a five on this hole; that's awful!"

I never say "a six," and I never *ever* say, "I'll probably three-putt!"

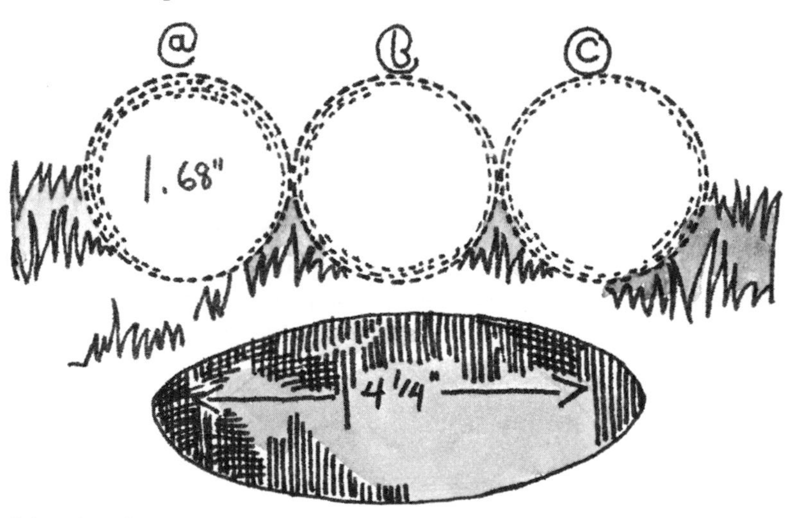

It's a rather terrifying thought, but as the above illustration shows, even when a putt is only one ball-width off-line, it has to fall into the cup from the side. If balls A and C were the width of a cigarette further off line, they would roll right by.

When I'm really a long way from the stick, instead of saying that I'm just going to lag it up, I pace off the distance from the cup to the ball and announce airily, "Now for another of my absolutely routine 47-foot putts."

It's a matter of forcing yourself to bear down. The big enemy for most golfers on long putts is that we are imprudently casual. We don't think we can sink it, and so we don't try—then we discover that not only did we not make it, but we didn't get close enough to make certain it will drop on the next stroke, either.

You can be totally inept off the tee, you can teeter along in and out of trouble on every fairway, you can be as insensitive as a frozen tooth on your approach shots, and you can still come out alive. But if you three-putt the greens, you are going to need an adding machine to keep your score.

Every high handicapper knows that good putting is important and all that jazz, but just to remind you of how important it is, let's isolate your putting from the rest of your game and look at it numerically. There are 18 holes to a round of golf. While the regulation number of fairway strokes can vary from as low as 30 on the "executive course," to as high as 37 or 38 on a long course, the number of putts never varies; it's always 36. No matter how big the greens, no matter how fast or slow or smooth or bumpy the surface, no matter how much the pitch and roll. Thirty-six. Period. So if you were to go out on a par-72 course and play heads-up bogey golf on every single fairway—then you get onto the greens and slop your way around averaging three putts on every one of them . . . your score would be *one hundred and eight.* But if you were to one-putt only one green and handle the other 17 in regulation figures—well within every duffer's capability—you would shave a big fat 19 strokes off that 108.

That's how important putting is.

As far as the stroke itself is concerned, most duffers make only one major mistake, and that is they try to knock the ball into the cup, rather than *sweep* it in.

You do not get good results when you swing the clubhead up in a pendulum stroke and bring it down into the ball like a croquet mallet. Instead, you must move the clubhead back along the grass, low, and bring it *through* the ball, lifting the clubhead no more than is necessary to keep it clear of the putting surface.

When the ball is stroked properly, in a smooth sweeping motion, it is sent toward the cup with a slight amount of topspin, so that it is rolling freely right from the moment of impact.

When it is improperly stroked, croquet style, the ball is rarely hit at, or just past, the bottom of the clubhead's pendulum arc. All too often it is hit while the clubhead is still coming down, so that the ball is pinched between the ground and the clubhead. It starts off with a little hop, then lands with a skid caused by the underspin of this pinching action.

The stroke is unpredictable, because all that "English" is constantly tugging at the natural capacity of a sphere to roll freely. The ball is pulled off line or it stops short, even though the stroke may have been quite brisk.

The unpredictability of the pendulum stroke sets up doubts in the mind, too. You find yourself saying: Do I let the clubhead hit the ball only with the force of gravity, or do I give it an assist? Usually you are trying to resolve these alternatives during the actual downswing—and the putting stroke is no place for indecision.

Invariably, this indecision makes you jab or punch at the ball. The blade comes down, touches the ball, and then jumps back. As with any jerky motion, it is difficult to control.

The proper putting stroke has natural follow-through built into it, so that when you sweep toward the hole, you merely let the momentum of the sweep expend itself naturally.

Here is how it's done:

As with the approach shot, the golfer determines with his practice strokes how fast the clubhead must be moving at the moment of impact to send the ball into the hole. He does not think of how hard he has to hit the ball—because, as always, the hitting of the ball is incidental, and the smooth sweeping swing is primary. Think of hitting the ball and you'll jab at it.

Because the putting stroke is so abbreviated, the amount of clubhead speed necessary is determined by both the length of the backswing and the force of the return swing. Some golfers like to take a fairly long backswing and generate forward speed gradually, others go back only a little way and come forward briskly.

Personally, I like the longer backswing, because if I don't have to be brisk in either direction, I can concentrate on being smooth. But either way, there is very definitely a follow-through.

Well, now that we all know what we're supposed to do, just what is the best way to go about it? The man who finds the single reliable answer to the question is going to get rich, because that is what every golfer in the world wants to know.

There are no points for style when it comes to putting. It's getting the ball to drop that counts.

There are all kinds of ways to execute the proper sweeping motion of the good putting stroke. All manner of grips and stances will do the job, and so will all kinds of putters. In the end, it's what feels right, and what produces results. All anybody can do is review the general rules and then develop a reliable personal style.

First of all, your body must be securely set. It mustn't move or sway, but it should be arranged so that your hands and arms are free to stroke the ball smoothly and squarely.

Some good putters stand up tall to the ball, others crouch over it. Some plant their feet very far apart, others take a narrow stand and turn their toes in until they're knock-kneed. Some line up square to the shot, others go very open, still others very closed. Sam Snead has tried hitting the thing between his legs.

I have seen some men arrange their elbows at right angles so that they stick out like chicken wings, and others who keep their elbows snug to the body. Most men like to get their eye directly over the ball (as I do), and there are some who tilt back and sight down the shaft as if it were a rifle.

There is also a bewildering, not to say bizarre choice of grips for you to choose from, including one in which the left hand is at the top of the shaft and the right hand is half-way down it.

All of them work. Not for everybody, but that isn't the point. From these various combinations of grips and stances and body positions comes a golfer's personal resolution of everyone's problem: how to make the ball take a predetermined line at a predetermined speed.

What seems to emerge, then, is not so much how you hold the putter, but whether the way you hold it allows you to keep the blade in a straight line while building up speed. This is something you can actually see and feel, in practice in your living room. And I believe it's best experienced without the ball. If you drop a ball on your broadloom and start trying to send it into grandpa's shaving mug, all you're doing is practicing your aim. Practice your stroke first, and when you can see that you can keep your blade straight, and feel that you can control its speed into the impact area, then try it out on a ball. I know that sounds a bit weird—as if practicing your aim were an unworthwhile occupation—but what I'm getting at is that a haphazard bull's-eye produced by any old kind of stroke doesn't really mean anything because it can't be reliably repeated. I would sooner miss the bull's-eye ten times out of ten, if I could send out every ball with exactly the same line and weight. All I have to adjust then is one direction, not ten.

It will help you to remember that if the body is to remain as steady as a rock throughout the swing, it must not be involved in any major way in lifting the blade of the club free of the grass to start the backswing. Therefore, when you're adjusting your grip to get the clubhead square, also adjust your up-and-down position on the shaft, so that only a fractional lift is required to clear the blade. If you get tugged offline just clearing the grass, it's tough to get back in line in time to hit the ball squarely.

Only when you have developed a consistent stroke can you discover your personal idiosyncracies regarding your ability to aim. Which stands to reason. If the stroke is sending the ball to the same place every time, it is doing its job. All that remains is to make your aiming ability pay off.

I went through a period, for instance, in which every stroke aimed at a cup ten feet away ended up approximately one cup-width to the right. The stroke was perfect, in terms of consistency, but I couldn't make a ball drop. It was mystifying because it was so un-erratic. Never left, always right.

The most reliable putting stroke is a sweeping motion. From address the backswing stays low along the grass, then comes through *the ball, rather than coming down on it.*

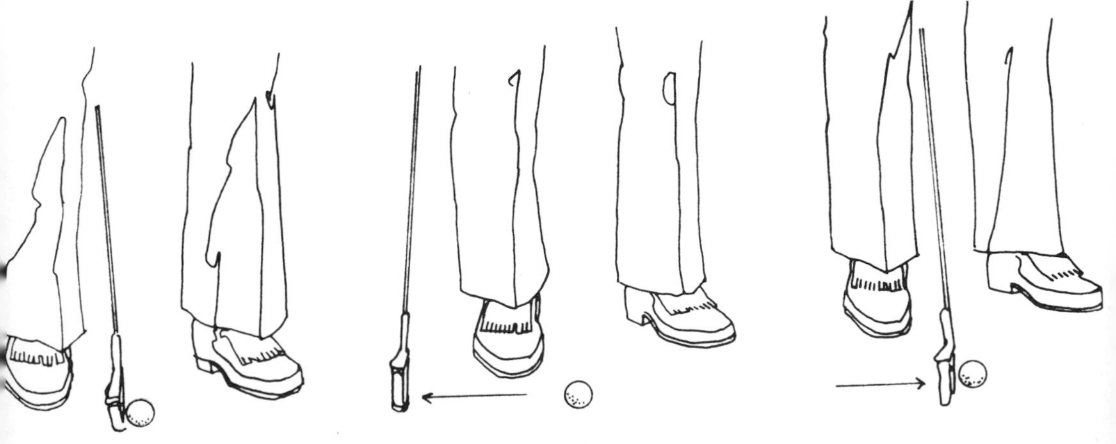

After a couple of hundred shots, I finally figured it out. I was hitting the ball squarely between my feet, but I was putting my weight on my left foot, as I recommend with all the other clubs. Because the path of the putter blade was straight, rather than coming around in an arc as it does in a regular golf swing, the slight inside-out path was shoving the ball three to four inches out of line at ten feet. As soon as I put some weight on my right foot, the path of the blade returned to square, and the ball dropped right in the cup.

This is the sort of thing you can fix only when you have a consistent stroke.

Finally, we come to the eyes. And there's only one instruction concerning them: Don't take them off the ball until you hit it, and then don't take them off where the ball was until your hear it drop in the cup.

No one can putt worth a damn if he takes his eyes off the ball. If you find that your gaze is still nervously jiggling around from ball to cup when you're ready to shoot, you're not ready to shoot.

With every putt, you must let the ball disappear right out of your field of vision; the most dangerous shot in golf is the putt in which you are so close to the cup that you can see it when you stand over the ball. Those little two-foot knee-knockers are murder. It takes iron concentration to resist the temptation to look at the hole instead of the ball. You can't believe you could miss that yawning crater of a cup from 24 inches away; and this kind of thinking brings on just the kind of carelessness which keeps the ball from dropping.

And it happens to everybody. Sam Snead loves the story about Clayton Heafner, the North Carolina pro who lost the Oakland Open to Jimmy Demaret by one stroke a few years back because he got careless and missed a short putt. Do you know how long that putt was? Three inches.

You can put in a lot of time on your living room rug perfecting your aim and your putting stroke, but as I'm sure you know, it doesn't solve all your problems when you step onto an actual green.

Your first problem is gauging the amount of beef each putt requires, and the only way I found to solve that one is to practice on the putting clock for a half hour and hope that my body will remember something when I get to the green. I notice a lot of golfers never bother. I also notice their putting doesn't knock me out, either.

On an actual hole, I pace off the distance first. I find that knowing it's "from here to there" isn't as good as knowing it's exactly 22 feet. When I know how far it is, I go behind the cup, scrunch down, and take a look at the lay of the land between the hole and the ball.

Then, as I walk back to the ball, I check the topography from the side. And finally, I do the same from behind the ball.

What am I trying to find out?

Most duffers, if they bother to give the lay of the land any attention at all, are trying to find out what direction the ball is going to have to start out on in order to reach the cup. That seems reasonable, except I don't think it's the best way to go about it.

I try to determine the line it will have to take in the last few feet, not the first few. In other words, work back from the cup, rather than forward from the ball. When you know the line the ball is going to have to take on the final approach, all you have to do is figure out in what direction and at what weight you have to hit it to get it onto that line.

Here's the rationale behind this backward approach.

As you have discovered already, it takes a fair amount of speed to send a ball uphill, and very, very little to make it go downhill. If the last three feet of the shot is uphill, it doesn't matter what the contour of the green is up to that point. But it does matter that it has enough speed at that point to climb up and into the cup. Conversely, if the final yard is downhill, you're not as concerned with the speed of the ball in its first three feet of travel as you are with giving it just enough weight to keep it rolling in the last three feet.

In other words, it is useless to have perfectly figured out how to negotiate the first 90 percent of a putt if you can't make it pay off in the last 10 percent. That's a frank admission that all you're trying to do is "lag it up."

When you have figured out how much steam it needs from three feet away to get into the cup, your next problem is the approach path. Again, you are not primarily concerned with the direction it starts out on, but the one it ends up on.

As you will have noticed, a ball will not hold a straight line on a sidehill traverse. Gravity will make it curl down. Therefore, you can't aim it on a straight line because it will lose momentum and stop short of the cup. You have to go well up the hill in order to be in the right position when the ball comes back down again.

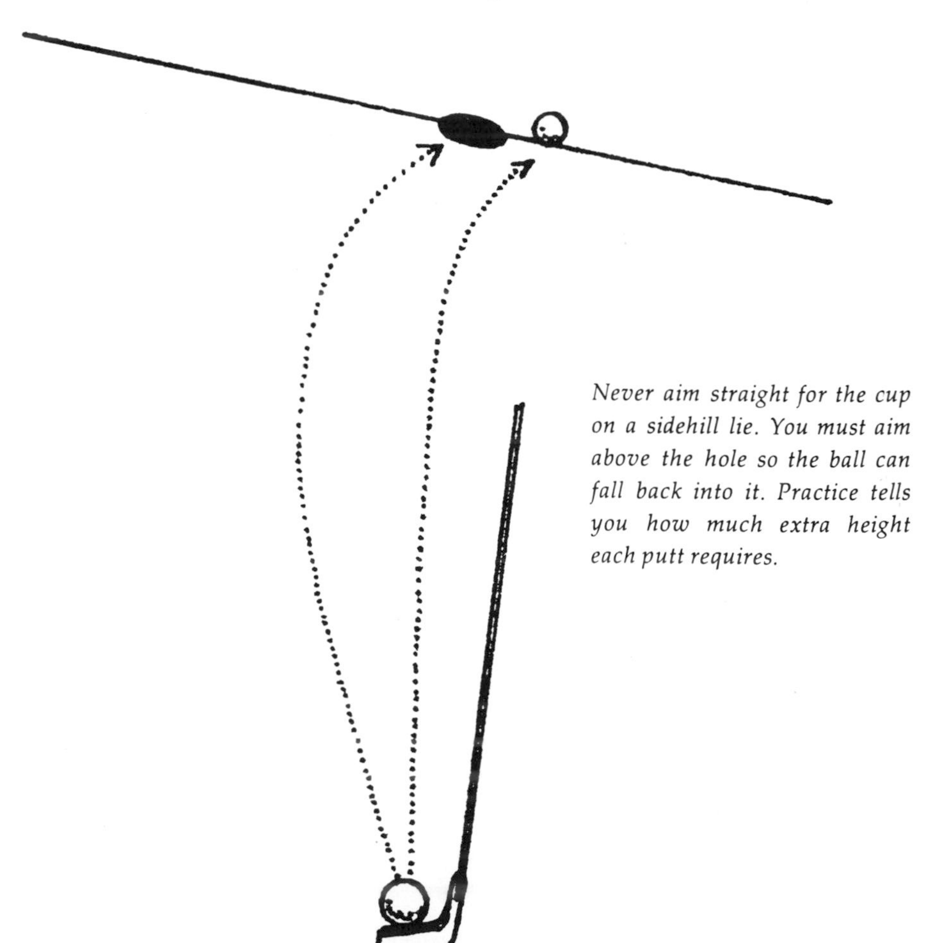

Never aim straight for the cup on a sidehill lie. You must aim above the hole so the ball can fall back into it. Practice tells you how much extra height each putt requires.

This is particularly apparent on short putts of let's say, five feet, where the ball is pin-high on a sidehill lie. If you give the ball five feet of weight aimed straight at the cup, it will fall off short. If you hit it briskly to try to overcome sidehill drag, you'll be a mile away if you miss or rim the cup. Your only solution is to aim up the hill with enough weight that when gravity pulls the ball down, it will encounter the cup while rolling slowly enough to fall into it.

With this five-footer, you can argue that you are thinking as much about the initial aiming line as the final drop line—or that you are taking your aim from the ball out and not from the cup back. But compound the problem and see what happens. Imagine you have another sidehill traverse added onto the first one—only the second one is in the opposite direction. In other words, your shot may have to take an S-shaped direction to find the hole. The only way I can figure out strokes like this is to determine the weight and the line of the last few feet and work back from there to the ball.

This means that on lots of greens I am not aiming at the cup at all. I am concentrating on that patch of grass, about the size of a nickel, over which my ball must roll if it's going to find its way into the cup.

Finally, if you're still uncertain, the next time you're faced with a problem putt, try this: In your mind, aim a shot directly at the cup, no matter what the lay of the land, but with enough weight that the ball would just nicely drop if the green were absolutely smooth. Then ask yourself, using all of the data you have been able to gather about the green's actual topography, just where that dead-straight shot would come to a stop. With a little practice, it shouldn't be long before you can see not only how, but where the topography would affect a straight shot. All you have to determine then is how much correction the shot requires to put the ball on a final line that will carry it into the cup.

Be wary if you're ten feet or more from the cup and you can't see a break anywhere. It's the rare green that's dead flat, and even if it is, the direction in which the grass is growing can affect your shot. A ball will go further if it is traveling with the grain, slower if it's moving against it, and will tend to curve away if it's moving across it. The way to "read the grain" is by standing at your ball and looking at the grass between it and the cup. If there's a shine on it, it's growing away from you and you'll be putting *with* it.

Both rain and dew make the green heavy. If you are playing in the early morning, or after a heavy downpour, expect that the wet grass will drag on your ball, and you'll have to hit it harder. In fact, if you don't have the honor, be smart and watch your opponent's shot. You can learn a lot about your own stroke from watching his.

SUMMARY

1. Approach each putt with confidence. If you think you can make it, frequently you're right. If you don't think you can make it, chances are you won't even try.
2. The proper putting stroke sweeps the ball into the cup, it doesn't swoop down and try to knock it in.
3. Follow through with every putt; never jab at the ball.
4. Adopt any grip or stance or body position you want to, as long as it allows you to keep your body steady and does not restrict a smooth, straight stroke.
5. At address, position your hands just a trifle low, so that you don't have to consciously lift the club to free the blade from the grass.
6. Keep your eyes on the ball until you hit it, then keep looking at where the ball was until you hear it drop into the cup. Never lift your head, never look at the cup until the ball completely disappears from your field of vision.
7. Learn how to read the green backward, from the cup back to the ball. Figure out where your ball has to get to roll into the cup, then worry about how to get it there.

The Nineteenth Hole

Over the 400 years and more that millions of men and women have been playing golf, there have probably been just as many millions of tips and pieces of advice crisscrossing the fairways. No one set of instructions can include all of this torrent of information, and I have not attempted to do it here. First, I don't know it all and I never will; and second, I wrote this book with the idea that I could help my fellow duffer get his game into bogey shape, and not much further. Beyond that, professional teaching is the answer. At this stage, to pile on too many more Do's and Don'ts would only confuse.

But there are a few loose ends that may still be intriguing you, and in this final chapter I will try to run through some of them, more or less at random.

● *What is the significance of Winter Rules?*

It all depends whether they are laid down by your golf committee to enable you to get as much enjoyment out of the game as you can in the off-months—early spring and late autumn—or whether they are laid down by the fellow who doesn't really want to learn the game. Basically, Winter Rules allow you to tee up your ball on a fresh patch of grass if you don't like its original lie, because it's in a puddle of mud or a bald spot stripped bare of grass by winter kill.

But it's a form of collusive cheating if you and your fellow players do it all summer long, because you are only willing to play the game if you are allowed to practically tee up your ball for every shot.

If you really are just learning the game, I think you should make it easy on yourself and move the ball to a fresh piece of grass if it lands on a bare spot. But once you feel justified in calling yourself a golfer, do yourself a long-term service and refuse the temptation to improve your lie. As a general rule, the only time you can touch your ball in normal play and not count it as a stroke is when it lands on the green. Then you can pick it up to clean it or remove it from another player's line. Otherwise, the only relief is under what are known as "Local Rules," which allow the ball to be moved in order to protect course property or to gain relief from unfair hazards. Landing in the long grass of the rough is not considered an unfair hazard.

● *What about stymies?*

The general rule is: If the obstacle in your path is alive, it can't be moved. You can't, for instance, have somebody hold up a branch while you're hitting out from under it. You can't mow down the long grass, or pull it up in handfuls, to clear your ball in the rough. You can, however, remove dead twigs and such, as long as you don't move your ball while doing so. (And if you do get into the long grass, take a practice swing near your ball to remind yourself that it's only grass, after all, and not railway spikes. Just remember to make sure you're in a solid body position, then keep your eye on the ball, hold the club firmly, hit down, and follow through.)

When you're in a sand trap, it's permissible to carefully remove the sand from your ball if it's buried—but only to determine that it really is your ball. No building up a little tee for yourself.

● *How do you play when it's really windy?*

If you are playing with either your driver or your fairway wood, forget about it. As a nonexpert, you're unlikely to get into trouble with overhitting off the tee or on the fairway, so the wind at your back is just a little extra help. If it's in your face, it's going to rob you of distance, but as a bogey player you have that one extra fairway shot to compensate. It's unlikely that you'll ever play in a wind so fierce that it will require more than your extra shot to cover the distance. Don't try to hit the ball harder, and if it's a tee shot, don't try to adjust your tee height. Only when you can really hit it reliably should you fool around with low teeing.

If you are on an approach shot, if the wind is at your back and blowing briskly, assume that it is going to add two clubs' worth of distance to your shot, and club yourself accordingly. Don't try to hit it softly and expect that the wind will give it wings.

If the wind is coming into your face, go up a club or two.

If the wind is coming across your shot, aim slightly into it and no more. The experts have all kinds of tricks to adjust for crosswind, but wait until you can break 90 before you begin to wonder what they are.

● *How do you handle an uphill lie?*

The shot will want to hook a little, so aim a bit right to compensate. Also, you have to lean into the stroke slightly, that is, weight definitely on the left foot, the ball well forward. Be sure you take a few practice swings to get the feel of the shift in balance, and be sure you can really trim the grass, because the easiest way to make the shot is to see where you trim the grass in practice, then arrange yourself so that that's where you'll hit the ball.

● *How do you handle a downhill lie?*

Everything is reversed. The shot will slice, so aim well right (because it will tend to slice more in a downhill lie

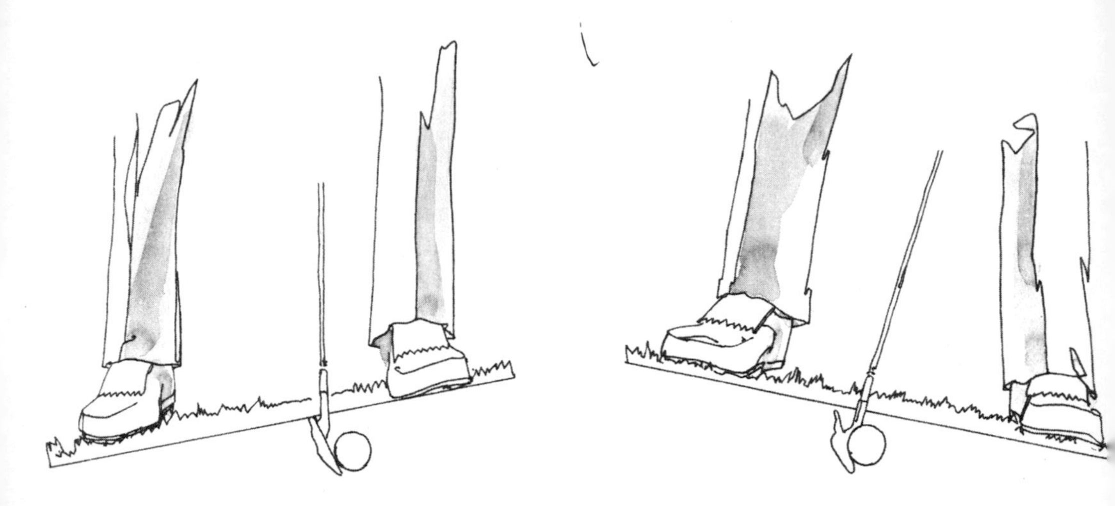

UPHILL AND DOWNHILL LIES. The trick is to make sure your clubface will meet the ball squarely in spite of the terrain. Closer to the left foot for an uphill lie, back toward the right foot on the downhill lie.

than it will hook in an uphill lie, in the experience of most beginners). The practice divot will be further back toward the right foot, so be sure to arrange yourself over your ball accordingly. One thing remains the same: the weight stays on the forward, or left, foot.

● *How about sidehill lies?*

They're no real problem if the ball is above your feet. Make sure you practice-swing enough to get the feel of where you will be encountering the ball, and make sure your weight is well balanced. As with the uphill lie, you'll hook a bit, so aim a bit right.

If the ball is below your feet, it isn't so easy. Sometimes you really have to scrunch down at the knees just to reach the ball. Also it will really tend to slice, so unless you've got lots of fairway, this is a place where you might consider altering your game plan and making two shots out of it. Remember, the essential thing is to keep the ball in play, and unless you're sure through practice that you're going to be able to hit it fairly smoothly, you might be well advised just to get the ball back onto flat ground again.

● *When should you take a penalty stroke?*

First, answer these two questions: Is the lie so difficult

that the shot from it is in danger of not reaching a playing surface? Is the best shot you can possibly expect to make going to make any material difference in advancing the ball toward the cup?

If there's any chance that you could end up with another bad lie, or that even if you get out you're not really saving a stroke, then there's no reasonable answer except to take the penalty. Most duffers feel they are committed to have a go at it, and that isn't wise.

Also, before you go sloshing through the water under a bridge, take a look at the Local Rules on the back of the scorecard. You may even find that you get relief from the hazard.

But remember, if the ball goes out of bounds, that isn't a poor lie, that's out of bounds, and it costs two strokes.

● *What's so illegal about grounding the club?*

What's so illegal about stacking a card deck? When you ground your club in a sand trap—purposely or innocently, it doesn't matter—you are clearing away the sand from behind your ball and in effect, you're teeing it up. The trap is a planned hazard; you got into it and you have to get out of it by your skill as a golfer.

Don't expect too many chaps to like playing with you if you are forever tamping down the turf behind your ball on the fairway, either.

● *When is a mulligan permissible?*

As far as I can interpret the rules, there really is a place where a mulligan is permissible—that is, if you mean by a mulligan a completely missed shot in which you don't even touch the ball. The game doesn't begin until you put the ball into play, so presumably you could miss it ten times off the first tee and it doesn't count. Once the ball's in play, though, every shot counts, whether you actually hit the ball or not. If the ball falls off the tee and strikes your driver, that doesn't count. But if you hit it or try to hit it, that's a stroke.

● *Just where do they measure the length of a hole?*

From the middle of the green, they measure backward along a line which bisects the fairway, sticking to the middle and not cutting corners. Then when they get to the teeing area, they put in a marker. Usually the tees are set a few yards back of that marker. But some courses don't have markers because the official distance was measured from the very back of the teeing area and somebody thought it would be a good idea to put the tees way forward so that you think you're hitting a really long ball. That's why I always like to march off the distance myself.

● *How many clubs do you really need?*

I know a guy who can break 90 with nothing more than a 2 iron. He also cuts his own hair and makes his own beer.

In tournament play, the legal limit is 14 clubs, which means even the pros can't take along everything they'd like. Basically, there are the woods, 1 to 5, and the irons, 1 to 10, plus the sand and pitching wedges and the putter. That's 18 clubs, but there are all kinds of variations on the standard weapons, such as the 11 iron and the 3½ wood, and you could probably end up with a couple of dozen if you wanted to. It seems to work out that the average golfer acquires the economy package: driver; 3 wood; 3, 5, 7, and 9 irons; plus the putter, for a total of seven. For the first season I would only add a pitching wedge to this assortment. It's a marvelous little tool for getting out of trouble and for recovery work around the greens. But as your skills increase, I would try to fill in the holes with the even-numbered irons so that you have all the irons from the 2 to the 9, plus the two woods, a wedge, and a putter. Being able to make a precise club selection gives you confidence, and anything that gives you confidence is money well spent.

● *What distance can you realistically expect from each club?*

If you can hit a smooth 9 iron about 100 yards (which is just about average), you can expect about 10 yards more per club up to the 2 iron. That is to say, on a flat fairway on a windless day, your average 7 iron shot will travel about 120 yards, your 5 iron about 140, and your 2 iron about 170. Your 4 wood has about the same loft as the 2 iron (20 degrees) and goes about as far. You can expect about a 15-yard difference in the woods, which means the driver should yield about 215 yards in the hands of a man who can hit 100 yards with his 9 iron.

None of these distances is absolute, merely an average. The important thing is that you should be able to get a little bit better than double the distance from your driver than from your 9 iron *without hitting any harder.* The club does the work, if only you'll let it.

● *How close should you stand to the ball?*

This is determined by several factors, including the lie of the clubhead and the length of the shaft. But if you can settle on one club which you feel you position reliably, figure the clubs up and down from it are not quite one ball width apart. That means the 9-iron shot is played about 15 or 16 inches closer to you than the drive.

● *What role does the ball play in your game?*

If you believe the ads, you will hit like Jack Nicklaus if you use $1.50 balls. And if you believe that, you probably suspect that only the 90- or 100-compression balls are hard enough to take your mighty stroke and that balls of only 70 or 80 compression are for sissies.

Well, let's be realistic. If you are still losing four or five balls a round, buy the cheapest balls you can get and ask for 70- or 80-compression balls. If the package doesn't show the compression rating, you can assume that it's 70, which is the quality of ball in general driving range use. Stick with it until you are starting to crack them out with real authority, because the lighter hitter seems to get better distance out of the softer ball. It's all a matter of rebound, and if you can't hit the high-compression ones hard enough to compress them, you won't get a full rebound and you won't get their true distance out of them.

Everybody hates losing golf balls—and everybody does it. But don't think of it just as money flying out of your pocket, because almost every time you lose a ball, it's a reminder that you tried something silly. If it stops you from doing it next time, it's well worth it.

● *How long will it be before you can shoot bogey golf?*

That may seem like a strange question, but a lot of beginners ask it. What I think they really mean is, how can I tell whether I am really improving.

As we all know, you can shoot a great game one day and a terrible one the next. You spend the evening congratulating yourself on having made the big breakthrough, then you go out the next morning and the roof falls in.

You might as well face it; it happens to us all and it's always going to happen. But a sign that you are improving is a narrowing of the range between your good and bad games, which is not the same thing as simply lowering your score. Obviously, once you get under 100 regularly, you are playing better golf than in the days when you were always over it. But you are also playing better golf when you shoot between 100 and 105 as against when you shoot between 95 and 120. No matter that your score is still up there in the triple figures; the important thing is that you seem to be pulling it all together, and breakthrough days are ahead.

Golf is a game which improves with the amount you play. The man who can get in 20 games in 30 days can't help but be miles ahead of the man who plays his games over one or two seasons.

If you are determined to improve, try to play as often as you can. And when you're not playing it, think about it. Golf is a thinking man's game as much as it is physical. It demands all the cool assessment you can give it.

Which brings us full circle. So let's leave it at this:

Keep your cool.

Keep your head down.

And keep trying.